The Town of Reading and its Abbey

1121–1997

Cecil Slade

To Margaret, John and Carol.

Acknowledgements

Sadly, Dr. Cecil Slade passed away in January, 2001 before this book went to print. However, he had completed the manuscript and it was his wish that I should undertake the publication of his work, the final result of which he would be justifyingly proud.

Cecil would have wanted to thank all those who helped in the production of this book. Firstly his wife Margaret for her help and encouragement during the early stages, together with the Berkshire Record Office, Reading Central Library and Reading Museum for making data available for study.

A special thanks to Professor Brian Kemp for reading the manuscript, suggesting minor changes and ultimately writing the Foreword. Acknowledgements are also due to Martin Marwood of MRM Associates Ltd. and Nicholas Battle of Countryside Books.

It is understood that Dr. Slade, where necessary, received permission to reproduce the illustrations. If this was not so we apologise for the oversight.

Luke Over M.B.E.

Contents

❖ ❖ ❖

Foreword

by

Professor Brian Kemp

I am delighted to write a Foreword to Dr Slade's excellent book on Reading and its abbey. There has been a crying need for such a book for many years, and Cecil Slade has now filled the gap admirably.

He traces the story from the foundation of Reading Abbey in 1121, through the heyday of its existence and its lordship of the town, on through its downfall in 1539 and the subsequent decay and destruction of its buildings, to the eventual rescuing of the remains in the 19th century and the laying out of the Forbury Gardens. The saga is a fascinating one, which the author tells with verve, affection and good humour, based on his immense learning and knowledge derived from nearly a lifetime's study of the records of abbey and town. It is Dr Slade's ability to see the history of abbey and town together, the one complementing and informing the other, that makes this book so valuable. Never before have the people of Reading (or elsewhere for that matter) had the opportunity to learn so much about the great abbey whose ruins remain in the town and about the close links between abbey and town both before and after the dissolution of the monastic community.

Dr Slade has read virtually everything available on the subject, whether published or not. He handles with equal ease a wide range of topics, including the constitutional relationship between abbey and town in the middle ages, the removal of building material from the dissolved abbey for various works in the area, the development of the Forbury as, among other things, a parade ground in the 18th century, the purchase of the ruins by the Corporation of Reading in the 19th, and, in our own time, the fate of successive, mostly ill-judged schemes to develop the Forbury Gardens, all of them fortunately fruitless.

The amount of information deployed is amazing. The book is a 'must' for anyone interested in the history of Reading. I commend Dr Slade's book most warmly to all inhabitants and lovers of Reading and its illustrious abbey.

Figures

I

A Relationship Established: 1121–1154

The foundation of the Abbey in 1121 was a momentous event in the history of Reading, which had already been in existence for some five centuries. The village lay in the extensive manor of Reading, a large agricultural estate that belonged to the king; but, probably by King Edward the Confessor (1042–66), the village was made into a borough. How this came about we do not know, but it was something very worth having, for under the reeve, the royal representative there, the inhabitants of the borough had considerable powers of self government and were no longer involved in affairs of the manor. However, Reading was a rather insignificant borough, far less important than Wallingford, then Berkshire's leading town. Its centre was the Old Market, later St. Mary's Butts, around which its few hundred inhabitants were concentrated. Its boundaries are shown on Speed's map of 1610, (see p 23), the first known map of Reading, but in 1121 it was far less thickly inhabited.

This year, 1121, saw the scheme of King Henry I (1100–35) come to fruition. Founding and endowing of abbeys was a widespread practice at this time, for not only was it an act of piety but founder's rights included solemn burial there, and prayers and masses for the founder's soul, all very important at this time and for centuries to come. In addition, a founder and his descendants could claim free hospitality during visits there. An abbey founded by a king would be expected to be large and wealthy; but in November 1120 the king's son and heir was drowned off the Norman coast in the White Ship disaster, when the ship, carrying many of England's young nobles, struck rocks and sank. It could well have been this calamity that impelled the king to a special act of piety in making his new abbey among the largest and wealthiest in the land.

A royal abbey had to be on royal land, but the king held vast estates, and it is possible that other sites were considered before Reading was finally chosen, but from the king's point of view the Reading area had several advantages. It was a convenient distance from both London and Windsor, whose castles were important royal residences, and on the main route to the west, thus excellently placed – certainly from the king's point of view – at a time when he and his court were almost always on the move. He had no special interests there that he needed to protect and Reading was well removed from Berkshire's one great abbey, at Abingdon. Two religious houses, Battle Abbey and Tutbury Priory did hold property in Reading, but Henry exchanged their holdings for land elsewhere.

The new Abbey was designed for 100 monks from the Cluniac Order, so-named from the Monastery of Cluny, in Burgundy. Here, in the tenth century had been established a reformed version of the monastic order established by St. Benedict in the sixth century, whose followers, the Benedictines, were known as Black Monks from the colour of their outer garments. The Cluniac Order, powerful and influential throughout Europe, was famed for its magnificent buildings, and the new abbey was to be a worthy addition. The actual site chosen must have delighted Cluny's representatives. The Cluniac Order did not seek solitude, and proximity to a town was an advantage, in providing for visitors not using the Abbey Guest House, workers for the abbey, income from rents and the many other services the town could provide, especially when it was so small and undistinguished as to seem to offer no threat to the authority of future Abbots. There was no existing religious house, but the memory survived of one in the past, possibly even on the actual site of the new abbey. Communications were good by land and water, the ridge between the rivers Thames and Kennet was spacious and healthy and was good building land. Just to the south of the town, uphill, at Whitley was a supply of good spring water, and there was river water close at hand for driving a mill and cleansing a toilet bloc. The chosen site, some thirty acres, part formerly Tutbury Priory's, part outside the town, seems to have been vacant, and there are no reports of dwellings demolished to make way for the new abbey. Maybe there had been no significant settlement in that area since the Danes had established their camp there in 870-1. Although it is doubtful whether any traces of their occupation survived into the twelfth century, it may be that the name, 'the Forbury', in the sense of an area, possibly fortified, in front of a town, and later used for the abbey's outer court, is a survival from this time.

It is impossible to appreciate local reaction when rumours about an abbey being built first spread in the town, or when surveyors and master masons arrived to plan the buildings, but once news of the sheer size of the abbey buildings spread, it must have been a major talking-point. There were certainly good reasons for welcoming it. Buildings would generate employment for considerable numbers of craftsmen, such as masons, smiths, plumbers, carpenters, tilers; and even if craftsmen came at first from elsewhere, labourers would be recruited locally from the start of operations. A wharf would have to be constructed for unloading the barges bringing Caen and other stone: carts and carters would have to be hired for carting sand, flint and timber from sites around; clay for roof tiles would be needed in quantity; and all the other things required for a major building project would have to be provided. An influx of money would

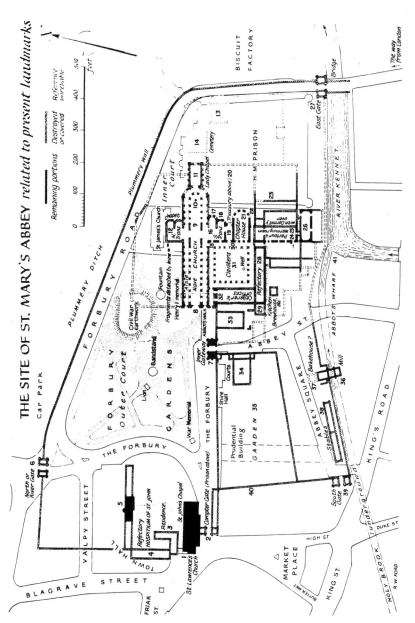

THE SITE OF ST. MARY'S ABBEY *related to present landmarks*

A modern plan of the Abbey

encourage service industries. Future thoughts would include the prospects that a Benedictine abbey gave for the employment of numbers of lay servants and maintenance men, and the spiritual benefits from a great abbey housing the relics of saints.

Most of these things would also benefit the leading men of the town, but among them must have been a division of opinion. Some must have stressed the advantages to themselves and the borough of being linked with what promised to be a very important man much involved with royal affairs – for all contemporaries knew the part greater abbots played in matters of state – and one certainly having royal favour. Some doubtless pondered on the superior jobs for which the abbey would need men of the middle class, while others could foresee an increased market for their goods and services. Others, however, must have felt that a lord on the doorstep instead of a distant king would greatly impede future steps to more power over their own affairs such as that already acquired by, for instance, the men of Winchester or Southampton, probably both known to Reading's leading men. It would, in fact, be a mistake to regard these leading townsmen as of one opinion, although their womenfolk, not directly involved in public affairs, were probably more free from doubts. The mass of the population cannot have had much interest in this aspect of things, for it mattered little to them whether king, abbot or leading townsmen were in charge; more relevant to them were the alms – left-over food and ale, and old clothes – distributed at the abbey gate.

There must have been considerable interest on 18 June 1121 when the first few monks formally took up residence, their numbers steadily increasing over the coming years. During those years the building of the abbey continued, with the imposing buildings in their new, off-white, stone becoming ever more dominant over the small wattle-and-daub and timber buildings of the town. A generation came into being that had never known a time when building works at the abbey were not taking place, for over forty years went by from the first arrival of the monks until the consecration of the church by the Archbishop of Canterbury, Thomas Becket, in 1164 in the presence of King Henry II and many of his nobles. A day such as that must have been long remembered by Reading people.

Meanwhile, the abbots had established a relationship with the town. It would seem they accepted that Reading was a borough with certain borough customs acceptable to the king and they simply slipped into his place. The king had granted the abbot considerable rights of law enforcement, and courts for this purpose were held by the abbot's representative in the gildhall in Yield Hall Lane. Reading's Gild Merchant that owned the Gildhall was a body of the town's leading men who had some say in the town's economic life and whose members were known as burgesses: each burgess paid a tax, *chepyangavel*, for the right to trade in the town and this went to the abbot, as did a payment from each new member of the gild. The burgesses continued to hold their meadow near the river Thames, in which to graze their cows, although there was some friction over the meadow to the east of it, later known as Abbot's Mead, the King's Meadow of post-abbey times. For the general maintenance of law and order the abbot appointed two reeves, soon to be called 'bailiffs', probably now, as later, from the local community and they might well have been burgesses of Reading. The abbot's hand, in fact, lay very lightly on Reading. He did not interfere with the gild, confining his activity to choosing, yearly, its warden from among its members; nor did he interfere with the customs – unwritten rules – under which property was held in the town.

It would be difficult to believe that there were no disputes between town and abbey during this first century or so of their mutual existence, especially as much at this time was based on 'custom' that allowed considerable scope for argument but around the mid-thirteenth century discord flared up. In 1244 there was a great disturbance at St. Albans, where the abbey bailiffs summarily tried and hanged a youth and, the writer adds,

> "likewise at Reading, on account of the killing of various people by servants of the abbey, whence the king was seriously moved against both houses"

So annoyed was the king with Reading abbey that he ordered the sheriff of Berkshire to take the abbot's considerable Berkshire estates into his own hand, although they were soon restored. It would seem likely that a popular riot was involved, possibly due to the abbot's trying to raise extra money, for around this time the king requested knights, free men and other tenants of the abbey to help reduce the abbey's debts by making a financial contribution. Reading men would have been among those asked, but no-one seems to have contributed, for the king soon wrote again, regretting no-one had complied and later, in June 1253, a similar request was made to help the abbey pay off its "manifold debts". This could only have made a bad situation worse, for earlier that year the abbot had complained to the king, who summoned the men of Reading before him to explain

> "why, armed, they repelled the abbot's bailiffs in Reading . . . and why by day and by night in the said town they have lain in wait for the abbot's bailiffs and servants and prevented them from carrying out their functions"

They could not justify their actions nor could they produce any evidence for rights they claimed were granted to them long before the abbey by King Edward the Confessor. It is small wonder that the king ordered the sheriff of Berkshire to see that the abbot's rights were upheld.

In all expectation this should have marked the end of the episode, but on 19 June 1253 the role of the sheriff was completely reversed, for he was now ordered by the king to act on behalf of the men of Reading. He was not to allow the abbot to move the town's market from its old site by St. Mary's church, nor to demand services other than those owed to the king's predecessors, nor to force Reading men to be brought before a court of law elsewhere than in their Gildhall, nor to take their gild and its possessions away from them. If the abbot was trying to change things to this extent, then Reading's leading men had every reason to complain. But their success went beyond this, for on 5 July a Royal Charter was granted "to the burgesses of Reading in the gild merchant there" giving them the right to buy and sell throughout England without paying any tolls or dues. In the past abbots had received similar charters on behalf of their men which, of course, included those of Reading; but now, in this, the first of Reading's many charters, the old privileges were granted directly to the burgesses and what must have caused much satisfaction to them was that the king recognised their gild. Of course, such favours did not come cheaply, and they cost the town £100. The money, a considerable sum at a time when meat cost ¼d. a pound, may well have swayed the king, who was permanently short of cash, but the really interesting point is that by now Reading's leading men were wealthy and sophisticated enough to challenge what they regarded as illegal activities by the abbot, one of the important men of the kingdom, and to bring the king, a lover of church and churchmen and a frequent visitor to the abbey, over to their side.

The sheriff, by the end of July, had done nothing to put things right, and he was chivvied by the king in no uncertain terms. One can only feel sorry for the sheriff, a local man, firmly ordered to confront the abbot, one of the most powerful men in the county and a leading figure in the church. He must have sighed with relief when town and abbey reached their comprehensive settlement in 1254, made before the king's court at Westminster. By it the abbot conceded the claims of the burgesses: that trading activities, including the corn market, should take place where customary; that the burgesses should have their gild merchant "for ever", together with their gildhall, 12 properties and their meadow, the Portmanbrook; and that courts of justice for Reading people should be held in the gildhall and nowhere else. The burgesses in their turn agreed that the rent they paid for the Portmanbrook should rise from 1d. to half a mark (6s. 8d.), and they withdrew their claim to the meadow at its head. Also that the trading tax paid by each burgess to the abbot should be 5d., and for new gild members the abbot should receive 4s. from the son of a gildsman and half the payment made by an outsider. Each year the abbot would appoint as warden of the guild a burgess acceptable to other burgesses, and the new warden would take his oath of office to both them and the abbot. The warden would freely hand over the gildhall key to the abbot when a court of law was to be held there, with all fines imposed going to the abbot. And, finally, that the abbot could levy an obsolete tax, the "tallage", whenever the king should tallage his own estates.

This was a most important document. Much that it contained had existed as unwritten custom, but these practices were now firmly established, with a copy of the document filed in the king's court; and it formed the basis of relations between town and abbey thereafter. It does not look as though either party gained significantly more power, but the burgesses had gained something of great importance to them: official recognition of their gild. The abbot mistrusted the gild as a potential rival authority in "his" town, and his attempts to attack its legality, instead of simply abolishing it, suggest it was in existence before he became lord of Reading. In practice, of course, abbot and burgesses usually co-operated, as over this agreement, which was a very civilized way of settling a fraught situation. The document containing it was what was known as a "final concord", the terms of which had to be agreed between the parties involved prior to coming before the king's court: it was not an imposed judgement. The whole episode clearly shows the wealth of the town and the worldly wisdom of its leading men, which leads naturally to wider aspects of social and economic relations between town and abbey.

Isolation and lack of travel in the middle ages are matters that have been greatly exaggerated. Many people, of course, did not move much beyond their immediate locality, but others did. Nobles moved from dwelling to dwelling, and to and from the king, important churchmen travelled on royal or ecclesiastical business, and all would be accompanied by considerable bodies of servants. Royal messengers, officials and servants were constantly on the move, likewise soldiers, traders, pilgrims, beggars, wandering scholars, entertainers, and so forth. Reading was an established town, well-placed on two important land routes that crossed here, and a river route, the Kennet, while a major river route, the Thames, lay just outside the town. These lines of communication, vital for the town's development, had existed long before the abbey. They had helped to make Reading a local market centre and thus had encouraged manufacturing, and on a wider scale had aided the development of the woollen industry in the town. Wool was of major importance in the economy of medieval England, and so in the prosperity of Reading, which remained an important wool town long after the fall of the abbey. The abbey's great contribution in this matter was to make the name of Reading well known, an obvious advantage for Reading's many merchants, and to encourage labour-intensive service industries by attracting visitors, most of whom would require food and lodging – very necessary when a day's journey was only a few miles – in addition to entertainment, replacing and repair of clothing and equipment, stabling for horses and so forth.

Kings were ceaselessly on the move and important events, such as Henry II's meeting with the patriarch of Jerusalem in 1185; or marriages, such as John of Gaunt's in 1359 or Edward IV's in 1464; or the meeting of Parliament in 1453 took place in this great royal abbey. But kings could routinely claim, and did, the hospitality that was included in founder's rights. The king who visited most was Henry III (1216–72) who came at least once, frequently three or four times, a year, and he might stay for weeks. A royal move was a major logistical exercise for it involved cartloads of his and the queen's household equipment and personal effects, and at least elements of the main departments of state and their officials with their equipment likewise being transported by cart; and the king would be accompanied by a train of attendants, and so it would be, although on a lesser scale, for nobles and bishops visiting or accompanying the king. So a royal visit involved the coming of many people and animals; and the abbey would not, nor be expected to, accommodate most of them, who would have to stay in the town or near around. No other king stayed as long or as frequently as Henry III, but kings did come, at times for weeks, as for example, in autumn 1340, spring 1360, early summer 1385, spring 1440.

But many people other than kings came to the abbey. The abbot was a great man, a spiritual peer, important in royal administration and high among the heads of monastic houses. Thus he was one to be consulted by leading men in church and state, none of whom would travel without followers. His church was magnificent and impressive, filled with works of spiritual art. It had amassed a first rate collection of holy relics, including the hand of St. James. The more important the relics, the more the number of pilgrims who would visit them. Pilgrimage was both a popular and a pious exercise with emphasis varying between holiday and spiritual aspects. Chaucer, in the fourteenth century, described an affluent, middle-class group moving from inn to inn between Southwark and the goal of their pilgrimage, Canterbury, and there is no reason to think that such did not happen in earlier times and with other holy places as their objective. People of any class went on pilgrimage. Nobles or their womenfolk so doing would personally receive the abbey's hospitality, but their escorts – and prestige demanded that an important noble should have a large escort – would often put up in the town, especially as the abbey guest-house would, for many, have a limited appeal. Other visitors were less desirable from the town's point of view: poor pilgrims; the sick, many from villages around, seeking cures from the relics; professional pilgrims, the palmers, who spent years, even a life-time, moving from shrine to shrine; or the needy, seeking the alms that religious houses dispensed. But even some of these might have simple needs to fill and pay for.

The influx of strangers was greatly swollen at times of the fairs. Permission to hold a fair was much desired, for the income it generated and for the unusual goods it attracted, because buyers and sellers would come from all parts, even overseas, and were free of the normal restrictions on trade. Three fairs had been granted to the abbot, each lasting four days. St. Laurence's fair of 10–13 August had been granted by King Henry I, but it died out after some one and a half centuries, in the reign of King Edward I (1273–1307). But the other two, St. James's fair on 25–28 July, granted by King Henry II (1154–59) and that of St. Philip and St. James of 30 April–3 May, granted by King John (1199–1216) flourished. On the Saint's Day, after whom the fair was named, there would be an impressive ceremony when the relics of the saint or saints would be carried in procession for all to venerate. Church authorities encouraged popular attendance by offering a number of so-called days of indulgence, giving, after death, remission from purgatory, to those visiting the relics of saints on their feast days: those coming, for example, on the feast of St. James could gain up to 386 days' remission, something very welcome when there was general belief in punishment in the after life. So the crowds at fairs were swollen by many whose aim was, at least partly, spiritual. All would view the procession of the relics, then turn to the business and entertainment of the fair, held in the abbey's outer court, the Forbury: the noise must have been very distracting for the monks in their buildings beyond the abbey's inner gateway. Fairs were often marked by unruliness and petty crime, and many Reading folk may well have been thankful that the abbot, rather than they, was responsible for law and order at such times, although possibly begrudging the abbey's receiving the rents from stalls and booths.

So the abbey's fairs were high-points in Reading's year. The goods there to be bought or even gazed at were very different from those sold on the town's stalls or at its weekly markets. Stalls selling goods or food and drink were there in abundance, but there were, in addition, entertainments of all kinds. That provided by humans, as jugglers, minstrels and glee-men, tumblers, buffoons, was rivalled by performing animals – dogs, monkeys, bears. Rougher entertainment included wrestling and cudgel-play while those of a milder disposition could enjoy puppet shows and even some play-acting. For the less fit, patent remedies were on sale, and every fair had its tooth-drawers. There was something for everyone. It was the opportunity for Reading's merchants to renew contacts, possibly even to arrange deals, with merchants from as far afield as France or the Low Countries, certainly to receive news of the wider world. Their women folk, with their much more limited lives, would have the pleasure of buying goods rarely available under normal circumstances. Local men engaged in manufactures, like pottery or leather goods, could get ideas from products made elsewhere. The lower classes, the great majority, led lives with, at best, small luxuries, and dominated by work; and a fair gave a chance to marvel at goods and entertainers, and for a few hours to enjoy a break from humdrum existence. Chance words at fair time with an outsider could open up vistas far removed from everyday life, but not only at fair time could this occur, for a pilgrim or king's carter or man-at-arms escorting a noble could tell of happenings far away, stories that probably lost nothing in the telling. These fortuitous outside contacts could, for a few of the enterprising and ambitious, doubtless lead to employment in the outside world: it would be very interesting to know, for example, how the three Reading men, overseas with King Henry III in Gascony in 1253, obtained their employment.

Within the town the abbey had an important part as an employer of labour. Obviously most Reading men and women were employed by their superiors in the town, but the abbey was certainly the largest individual employer. Senior monks were responsible for various aspects of abbey administration: the almoner, for example, was responsible for the distribution of alms, the infirmarer for running the infirmary for sick monks, the cellarer for the provision of drink, the sacristan for the interior of the church; and there were many others. Each of these was aided by superior lay servants, under whom would be many humbler laymen working in brewhouse, bakery, kitchen, mill, stables, infirmary, laundry and garden. Men would be needed at the abbey wharf on the river Kennet where water-borne supplies for the abbey were landed, likewise carters to bring agricultural produce to the abbey from its nearby manors. Cleaners would be needed in considerable numbers, especially as cure of illness by sacred relics frequently involved extensive vomiting, usually in the abbey church. Then so vast a complex needed a constantly active staff of stonemasons, carpenters, smiths, plumbers, glaziers and tilers, all with their labourers, whose work could only increase as the buildings aged, or on special occasions like the reflooring with tiles of the main buildings in the thirteenth century, or the building of the Lady Chapel in the early fourteenth. There were also the pilgrim badges, showing the scallop shell of St. James, to be made, likewise *ampullae*, small sealed flasks, for holy water, and other pious emblems it was hoped visitors would purchase.

So in these ways the abbey benefitted the town, but over some matters the verdict is not so clear. Food and old clothing given as alms at the Abbey Gate relieved necessity among poor townsfolk, but would also attract the poor and professional beggars from outside the town, both undesirable from the town's point of view. In around 1130 Abbot Anscher established a Leper Hospital in the abbey, but most of the inmates probably came from outside Reading. The almshouse established by the abbey, close by the west gate, was designed originally for twenty six aged and poor men and women. This relief must have been welcome to the few receiving it, but towns without abbeys managed to set up almshouses; certainly, when the abbey almshouse lapsed, in the fifteenth century, John a Larder, a Reading man in royal service, endowed a row of almshouses along the edge of St. Mary's churchyard quite independently of the abbey. Nor does the abbey seem to have done much about education in Reading. The abbot had been given control over schools in Reading, but the abbey's schools there that receive very occasional mention seem insufficient for providing the sons of merchants and professional men with their necessary education; and inhabitants of prosperous towns without abbeys had no difficulty in establishing schools.

It could well be that one of the abbey's greatest gifts to Reading was intangible. To most people living in the middle ages life in this world and the life to come were closely linked. Saints and martyrs in Paradise were freely invoked to help remedy the sickness and misfortune so prevalent in the present world, where medical skill was limited and expensive, the folk remedies on which most people relied were, even if cheaper, at least as limited, and the strong constantly oppressed the weak. Supernatural help was often the only hope, especially as it was generally held that illness – and even misfortune in general – was divine punishment for sin. Appeals to saints to intercede on ones behalf could be made anywhere, but it was generally held that such appeals were far more effective when made in the presence of some bodily or personal relic of the saint being invoked. The abbey had a splendid collection of some three hundred. In first place, as has been said, was the hand of St. James the Greater, the Apostle, but among the rest, for example, were blood and part of the skull of Archbishop Thomas Becket, murdered in his cathedral in 1170, the skull of St. Philip, the jawbone of St. Ethelwold, the well-known English saint, pieces of the true cross and, for those of simple faith, relics of the Virgin Mary including her hair and her belt. Reading people must have found hope, or at least consolation, from prayer to a saint before his or her relic in the great awe-inspiring church.

However, there can be no doubt of the importance of the abbey in Reading's economic life, for right until its end it provided employment for a number of local people, and continued, even if on a reduced scale, to attract visitors to the town. Nor can it be doubted that in the early days the privilege granted to the abbot, that his men could trade throughout England without paying trading taxes, benefited his men of Reading. However by the mid thirteenth-century Reading men were wealthy and confident enough to approach the king to obtain this privilege for themselves, and to defend it thereafter. The town's favourable trading position on roads and rivers, especially its being an outlet for the major wool-producing area to the west, enabled it to take full advantage of the early help given, even if incidentally, by the abbey, so that it could thereafter surge ahead on its own. It might have been that the town produced men of unusual ability: certainly by the early fourteenth century Reading had surpassed all other Berkshire towns, paying at·least twice as much in royal taxes as any other, whether Wallingford, the leading Berkshire town in Domesday Book, Windsor, with its great royal castle, or Abingdon, a long established town with a similar major abbey. Contemporaries, whether townsmen or abbot, might at times have felt dissatisfied with the relations between town and abbey but, from the point of view of history, a fair balance seems to have been struck.

The Medieval Abbey from a model

II

A Mature Relationship: 1255–1539

For almost two hundred years after the agreement of 1254 there is only a little information concerning relations between the town and the abbey, but in Reading the abbot's powers were limited and so unlikely to provoke popular trouble and riot, as happened at Abingdon in 1327 or Bury St. Edmunds in 1381. A major cause of popular discontent in such cases was when corn had to be ground at the abbot's mill and, maybe, bread baked in his oven, but there was nothing like this or, indeed, anything in the abbot's powers in Reading liable to provoke the mass of the population. The leading men of the town were as concerned as the abbot in the preservation of order, for disorder was costly and could provoke unwelcome visits from the king's judges; so although disputes arose at this level, they were kept to this level, and the mob was never involved.

There were, however, various points at issue and one was the title of Reading's leading burgess. The agreement of 1254 called him the "warden of the gild" but in 1301 the town received a standard royal writ, addressed to "the Mayor and Bailiffs of Reading", ordering the election of two members of Parliament. Thereafter the burgesses always used the title of "Mayor" for their leading dignatory, as did royal officials when communicating with Reading, but the abbot continued to refer to the "warden of the gild" – the change of title made no difference to his powers or the way he was chosen. The abbot was correct in law, but he had no success in abolishing the new title, which he refused to use, and the matter continued to rankle. The burgesses were not so successful over the tallage, an out-of-date tax that the agreement of 1254 allowed the abbot to impose when the king did. In 1302 and again in 1359, when the king was very short of money, he tallaged his lands, and the Abbot seized his chance to do likewise in his lands, including Reading. The Borough protested, probably more in hope than expectation, but the abbot had right on his side. Twice during these years the abbot's activities were the subject of royal inquiry, probably following complaints from the town, but the matters seem very trivial. In 1376 it was reported that, when the abbey should, twice a year, distribute to the poor alms of a "sufficient" loaf, and herrings worth 1½d. (c½p.), only ¾d. worth had been given; also that the abbey had not appointed a chaplain to St. Edmund's chapel for ten years.

This chapel, founded by a hermit in the early thirteenth century, was on the west fringe of the town, just beyond the end of later Friar Street, and nothing seems to have been done, for there was a similar complaint in 1413. On this occasion, the abbot was also accused of withdrawing the chaplain from the Chapel of the Holy Ghost on Caversham Bridge and of closing the leper hospital in the abbey. It rather looks as though the abbey was trying to save money.

The main recorded dispute of the fourteenth century involved not the abbot but his steward. Law and order in Reading were maintained by the abbot's bailiffs aided by two constables. These were elected yearly, were unpaid and were usually burgesses, very often senior ones. They were not mentioned in the 1254 agreement, but their election and appointment – a joint affair between abbot and gild – did not normally cause trouble. The steward in 1391 was Reginald Sheffield, a local man, engaged at times in royal administration, and he had even been one of Reading's two members of Parliament in 1376, implying that he was a burgess. The constable involved was William Shortwade, a prominent burgess engaged in the cloth trade, and three times member of Parliament for Reading. At this particular moment he was overseas, and so can hardly have been doing his job. When the steward dismissed him, the mayor and burgesses refused to elect a replacement, and when the steward chose one and forced him to take the oath of office, the mayor and burgesses refused to accept him. Even here though the squabble did not spread outside the tight group of burgesses, for the steward's unwilling nominee was John Harald, a burgess, who had already served as member of Parliament for the borough and was, in 1396, to become mayor. The matter came before one of the king's judges, the Reading men supporting their case by claiming pre-abbey rights, including that of choosing constables but the whole affair blew over and the abbot avoided getting involved.

Nor did he get involved in new national developments that involved the town. The reign of King Edward I (1272–1307) saw major steps in the development of Parliament and continuously, from 1295, Reading returned its two members, chosen by the burgesses. There is no record that the abbot interfered in this: in any case, as a spiritual peer, he sat among the Lords, then the more important element in Parliament. Another development in the fourteenth century was the emergence of new royal taxes, and the responsibility for appointing people to assess and collect them in the borough was the gild's, more senior members being chosen for these unpaid but responsible tasks. In both these matters, of Parliament and taxation, royal authorities corresponded directly with the town, with no reference to the abbot who, in 1379, seems to have avoided an attempt by the town to involve him in contributing to taxation.

For most of the time, then, things seem to have run smoothly, with problems obviously settled by negotiation. A good example of this occurred in 1405, when a formal agreement was made for the passage of "botes (boats) and other vessels callid showtes" from the mouth of the

A reconstruction of Reading Abbey Wharf in the 15th century: from a diorama in the Museum of Reading

river Kennet past the abbey wall and lock to High Bridge, by the site of the town wharf, between sunrise and sunset. Payments due to the abbey were laid down, damage to abbey property was to be made good, and no-one on the boats was to

> "make any play, riott or noise that myght turne to the prejudice, damage or dis-ease of the said abbot and convent."

Clearly something had gone wrong, and the town in effect assumed responsibility for behaviour by boats' crews. A very unexpected co-operation between town and abbey occurred in 1349 when Bartholemew de Burgherssh, one of King Edward III's important men, accused the abbot, some monks and some Reading men, of carrying away his goods and assaulting his men and servants in Reading. No more is known, but one can suspect that there was a lot more to this than simple robbery.

The last century of co-existence between active abbey and town was marked by a series of disputes between them, not necessarily more than previously, but more records happen to be available. The first of these concerned stalls used by 'foreign' (i.e. non-Reading) butchers, the so-called 'outbutchery' in Broad Street. The gild regarded this as its property, maintained it and took rents from the stall-holders. But Thomas Henley, who became abbot in 1431, clearly thought the gild had exceeded its rights, and he took the stalls into his own hands, claiming that they were "repaired, made and sustaynid" by him. The gild, however, claimed that it was responsible for such things, and had paid rent to the abbot for the stalls. In the face of such sure claims it is hard to see who was right, and it would seem that neither side was prepared to compromise. This, and probably other disputes, continued over the next twenty years, culminating in the time of Abbot John Thorne I (1446–86) in a burst of legal activity. This involved the mayor and other burgesses in journeys to London and elsewhere, and in considerable expenditure. The King's Council was contacted at various times, and once 6s. 8d. (33p.) was paid to "le foteman" of the lord king, a considerable sum when a day's wage for a labourer was 4 d. (less than 2p.). The burgesses engaged the legal services of Lyttleton and Wimbish, two of the eminent lawyers of the day. There was a formal meeting between abbot and burgesses, and the abbot's lawyer was shown "the articles of the gild". Somebody in high authority must have given a ruling in favour of the abbot, for in 1452 this legal activity virtually ceased, and from that year income from the outbutchery no longer appeared in the gild's accounts. In fact, the income was lost to the gild until 1525 when a sensible compromise was reached.

Abbot John Thorne I became involved in another dispute with the gild, this time over the mayor's mace. At a time when outward show was important, the mayor wished to have, as many mayors elsewhere had, a mace borne before him to enhance the dignity of his office. King Henry VI, during a visit to Reading at some time before 1458, gave permission for the warden of the gild to have a mace borne before him, providing

"that it be not prejudicall unto oure church and monasterie of Redyng".

On Friday, 3 November 1458, the mace, made at a cost of 3s. 4d. (c16½p.), was produced by the mayor at a gild meeting but very soon another communication was received from the king, accusing the mayor of having used the mace "otherwise than was or is according to our entent", and ordering that he should not be known otherwise than as "keper of the Gild of Reding". The reason given by the king was that the grant was contrary to the abbey's long-established privileges, for only the abbot's bailiff in the borough was entitled to have two tipped staves – these would, of course, be carried before him on formal occasions. As this latest royal letter referred to "shewing of evidence", it would seem that the abbot had made formal complaint to the king. So the mayor lost both his mace and his usurped – as it appeared in the abbot's eyes – title. Although town documents continued to refer to "the mayor", the abbot had won. His triumph lasted for nearly thirty years, a triumph that must have grieved the burgesses.

In 1462 a small group of senior burgesses, headed by the "mayor", was chosen to deal with certain matters at issue between abbot and burgesses. This was obviously an important occasion, but nothing more is known about it. Probably nothing resulted for in 1481, still in the abbacy of John Thorne I, an extensive catalogue of complaints was presented to King

Edward IV (1461–83) by "the town and the country" when he came through Reading. The complaints related to matters old and new. Caversham Bridge, High Bridge and other bridges throughout the town, the responsibility of the abbot, were neglected, as were St. Edmund's chapel, "now made into a barn", and the chapel of the Holy Ghost on Caversham Bridge. St. John's almshouse, just north of St. Lawrence's church, near the abbey's west gate, for widows of former office holders in the town, likewise their "fair chapel", had been empty since 1465 or before, the abbot taking and retaining the income from the lands with which it had been endowed. The chapel and leper hospital of St. Mary Magdalen, within the abbey precinct, had been demolished, its income being likewise appropriated by the abbot. The king instructed the bishop of Salisbury, in whose diocese Reading lay, and who was responsible for its good order, to investigate; and he, after an extended visit, departed

> "full ill content not only for this (i.e. the matters in the petition), but, as is said, for many things misordered in the place by the wilfulness of the said abbot and his accessories"

Unfortunately the bishop shortly died, and even many years later nothing had been done. So the grievances remained to annoy the burgesses and other townsfolk and, conversely, the very fact that a complaint had been made doubtless annoyed the abbot.

So both sides already had cause for complaint before 1487. By then, great changes had taken place in national affairs, for in 1485 King Richard III had been killed at the Battle of Bosworth, and Henry Tudor, King Henry VII, now occupied the throne. In the early years of his reign he needed all the support he could get, including that of Parliament. Towns, whose leading men desired the law and order that peace brought, were potential supporters, and many, like Reading, sent two members to Parliament. So for the Parliament of 1489 John Williams, one of Henry VII's professional administrators became, in 1488, a member of the gild merchant without making a payment for the privilege, and was the same day chosen as one of Reading's two members of Parliament, the other being another royal servant, previously admitted to the gild. Reading thus obliged the king, an action seemingly connected with a charter granted by the king in August 1487.

This charter went far beyond any Reading had received in the past, for earlier royal charters had simply confirmed that of King Henry III in 1253, freeing Reading burgesses from paying trading taxes throughout England. This new charter confirmed the old grant, then dealt with fresh matters. It gave the mayor judicial powers over all cloth traders and workers in the town, the abbot's only involvement being to receive any fines. This by-passing of his authority was, from the abbot's point of view, bad enough, but the charter addressed "the Mayor and Burgesses of Reading" who were allowed "in every year for ever" to elect, in their gild hall, two sergeants-at-mace "to serve and attend upon the mayor". This complete reversal of King Henry VI's ruling was a significant triumph for the burgesses, for the highest authority in the land now formally approved the mayor's title and mace, and the grant in perpetuity – "every year for ever" – quite undermined the abbot's claim that the gild existed only by his favour.

The abbey, meanwhile, had been distracted by its abbot's death in 1486, but no burgess could have been in any doubt concerning some counter-action by the new abbot, John Thorne II. He had not been long in power when he clashed with Richard Cleche, a wealthy draper and the first of his family to be a burgess. He had been mayor in 1486–7 and so had played an important part in obtaining the new charter. He seems to have relied on the abbot's word, for according to an old memorandum, the abbot promised to implement its terms, and got Cleche to take letters to his, the abbot's, "lernyd councelle at Londone". Cleche thought all had been resolved, but a fellow-burgess warned him in strong terms not to trust the abbot's word. This was a wise warning, for not only did the abbot fail to carry out his promise, but in 1488 he chose Cleche for mayor, although he was not one of the three put forward, "to his great cost and charges". It would seem that personalities were clashing, for, in a later lawsuit, the abbot stated that Cleche

"hath of long time borne grudge and malice to the said abbot and his monastery".

and Cleche's denial was by no means convincing.

Cleche as a newcomer may have been dissatisfied with existing arrangements between town and abbey, but he was not alone, having the support of some 20 other burgesses, some very senior. In 1490 one of these, John Baxter, became mayor, actually for the fourth time, and his year saw a flurry of legal activity, including four petitions to the king, and hospitality for visiting lawyers. However matters escalated in September 1491, when it was time for the abbot to select the warden from the three put forward by the burgesses, and he refused; but after six months he chose another burgess, Cristin Nicholas, as warden for the rest of the year. The abbot's lawyers had doubtless told him to stick to the letter of the 1254 agreement, which said nothing about three candidates, while the burgesses were advised to maintain existing practice. This impasse continued for the next five years, with the burgesses choosing three, the abbot refusing to appoint. It cannot have helped the situation that each year at least two of the three put forward belonged to the anti-abbot faction. To concerned outsiders, the situation was most unsatisfactory, but despite the "friendly consultation" the king ordered on the parties, and despite

"the judges taking upon them right great pain and labour immense and many times calling both parties before them"
there was no solution in sight.

How the gild got on without its head is not known, but the situation was clearly most unsatisfactory, so in October 1496 a group of twenty-one burgesses – over thirty stayed away – took matters into its own hands, and elected the hard-line John Baxter as master of the gild. Possibly the burgesses were not as rash as it would appear, for among those voting for Baxter was "in the first John Williams Esq", important in the king's service. Some burgesses were clearly not happy with the way things were going, so all were ordered to swear to maintain the gild liberties and ordinances, and to obey the master of the gild as formerly they had obeyed the mayor. The year of office of Baxter's successor, Cristin Nicholas, again elected by the burgesses, saw considerable payments made to "men of the lawe and Councelle", and John Williams, now Sir John, received gifts and entertainment at the Bell Inn but it was under Nicholas's successor, Cleche again, that matters escalated. In December 1498 the burgesses agreed

> "that if there be any burgess do otherwise than concerning by his oath he ought to do, then he be put out of this Gild and openly shamed. Also if any burgess take upon him to take any office as Constable or Warden except they be of the election and choice of the Mayor and his fellow burgesses, that any of them doing so at any time be put out of the gild".

and on the same occasion he discharged the two constables appointed by the abbot and replaced them with his own.

Such activity was on the fringe, or even beyond the bounds, of legality, and the abbot sued a group of burgesses, including Cleche, on the grounds that he, the abbot, should appoint constables and was responsible for law and order in the town. Cleche asserted that the abbot had appointed constables contrary to custom, and that during the approach to Christmas

> "misruled people daily increased and continued, as carders, dicers, hazarders and vagabonds, and many other unlawful games in the said town were used by night as by day"

for the abbot had appointed

> "simple and perjured persons to the office of constable which in no way regarded the good rule of the said town"

In actual fact, the abbot's appointees, so summarily dismissed, were both senior burgesses, and one of them, John Turner was, in 1503, to become mayor. Their willingness to serve the abbot shows that not all burgesses went along with Cleche. The abbot further accused him of "riotusly" breaking the stocks – they stood in the Market Place – and handing over new keys to the constables he had appointed. Cleche retorted that the abbot's representatives had refused to hand over the keys when repairs were needed; and to emphasize his claims he spent, during his year of office, 4s. 3d. (c21 p)

> "for thamending of the stockes, bordes, lockes, boltes, nailis, workemanship"

However, despite this apparent escalation of the quarrel, things began to improve. Customary payments had continued to be made by the gild during these years, but in Cleche's term of office in 1498 – 9 an unexpected gift was sent from gild to abbot

> "Item, 2 pike and 3 perches sent to my Lord of Reading 5s. 6d. Item for 2 couple of capons given to my Lord of Reading 3s. 8d."

and in 1499 there was a significant improvement, when the abbot chose Cristin Nicholas from the three put forward by the burgesses. He was chosen by the abbot "of his special grace" that is, without prejudice, while a legal decision was pending, but thereafter the abbot selected the master of the gild in the normal way from the three candidates. The situation must have been rather uncertain until 1507 when a settlement was reached, but there is no record in these years of trouble between gild and abbot, who dropped his lawsuits and, in fact, in most years picked a former hard-liner as warden or master of the gild. But in 1507 an official ruling was in the offing, and it is significant that the burgesses included Cristin Nicholas among the three candidates, and the abbot chose him. He wisely associated two former hard-liners, including Cleche, with himself in the arbitration process, and his journeys to London culminated in "necessary expenses at Westminster divers times", involving the very considerable sum of £13 6s. 9d. and, obviously, a lot of work.

It would have been difficult for either party to dispute the verdict of four such arbitrators as two prominent judges, the Lord Privy Seal and the King's Chamberlain. The judges first decided the main legal point, with the result that they

> "affirmed the said Mayor and Burgesses of the said Gilde Merchant to be corporate"

The burgesses had long been claiming this, so the decision was most gratifying. All four arbitrators then pronounced that the keeper of the Gild Merchant – the term "mayor" was carefully avoided – was to be chosen by the abbot from the three nominated by the burgesses, otherwise "all other things and articles" in the agreement of 1254 were to be "firmly observed and kept". They also pronounced on the way in which town and abbot should participate in the election of the two constables and their subordinates, the ten wardmen – two to each of the wards of medieval Reading. The arbitrators also tidied up the matter of the trading tax, which allowed burgesses and their widows to trade freely in the town: "from henceforth" they could, without extra payment, set up stalls "in the void grounds of the said town", although stalls blocking streets or annoying inhabitants were to be dealt with by the abbot's bailiffs. This was a fair settlement of what must have been a matter sufficiently serious to come before the arbitrators but they refused to pronounce on the other stalls, those of the outbutchery, requiring more "evidences" to be shown.

This episode can be examined in some detail, thanks to the survival of a scatter of documents that gives us some idea of persons, motives and methods. It is the one episode in the relations of town and abbey where the human element can really be seen, and so is a useful reminder that people lay behind all those other episodes so factually and fragmentarily recorded. Even here though there is no evidence to tell whether either side regretted the tension and expense of these years. However, the outcome does suggest that with average good will on both sides a solution would have been within easy reach, for the arbitrators' award was essentially a limited tidying-up of the status quo, but one name frequently occurs during these years, that of Cristin Nicholas. He was possibly a "bere-brewer", as was Nicholas Nicholas, his son and, later, burgess. He himself had not become a burgess until 1488, thereafter, in 1489, playing a small part in assessing a tax. However from 1491, as we have seen, both abbot and burgesses utilized his services, and he seems to have played a key role in resolving the situation: his being selected in 1504 as member of Parliament could well have been connected with negotiations in London. It was in 1507, during his fourth time as mayor that the arbitrators' decisions were received, and the copying of their decree in the Corporation Diary:

> "Item payed to the mayers clerke for wryting of the drafte into the Gildhall boke made by the Juges vi d."

must have given him a sense of something well done. He did not long survive his achievement, dying during the winter of 1508–9. He certainly deserves a place among Reading worthies.

There remained a few loose ends to be tied up. There was no further trouble over the mace, and the matter of the stocks was quietly dropped. In 1508 abbot and burgesses, possibly prodded by the judges of the arbitration award, sorted out immediate matters concerning constables and wardmen but when, in 1509, the abbot, still John Thorne II, refused to select a mayor, the current mayor, one of the former hard-liners, simply carried on. The dispute seems to have been over the abbot's share of the payment by new burgesses. Burgesses had been elected during the troubled years and subsequently, but the abbot refused to acknowledge them, so now there were only five acceptable to both sides. The matter was settled by five members of the king's council, who precisely defined the process for electing burgesses, and by December 1510 some 40 new ones had been sworn in. Probably the Abbot here was in the wrong. He was certainly so over choosing the mayor, the five counsellors ordering him to select from the three already put forward. Abbot John Thorne II did not foster easy relations with the burgesses.

The last episode in the affair occurred in March 1511 when the mayor and burgesses showed their proud possession, "the kinges grete chartere of the liberties of the Gild Merchaunte of the burghe of Redynge" to various judges and it was "in all thynges allowid". This was probably the abbot's last attempt, and the rest of his time as abbot seems to have passed peacefully, as far as relations with the town were concerned, as did that of Thomas Worcester, his short-lived successor. Under the next abbot, Hugh Cook Faringdon (1520–39) the long drawn out dispute over the outbutchery was, in 1525, settled by arbitration. Both parties agreed on the two arbitrators, whose very detailed award gave the outbutchery and small areas of "voide grownde" to the "mayor or keeper" and the burgesses, who would pay an agreed annual rent to the abbot. There is no information on whose initiative this came about, but it seems a fair, even an obvious, solution to a previously intractable problem. The old positions were maintained over "mayor" or "warden of the gild", but there is no evidence of further discord.

So all outstanding issues between burgesses and abbot had been settled, and a period free of major discord could have been anticipated but events far beyond Reading and Reading's abbey were beginning to influence local affairs. The matter of the annulment of the king's marriage to Catherine of Aragon had spread far beyond its original scope, and in 1534 King Henry VIII had become Supreme Head of the church in England. Their wealth and influence made abbeys obvious targets for the king and his many avaricious followers. Attempts by Reading Abbey to buy the favour of Thomas Cromwell, the king's all-powerful minister, failed, and by late summer 1539 the abbot was accused under the 1534 Treasons Act and imprisoned in the Tower. In this time of tension throughout the land, of spies and informers, rumour and counter-rumour, Reading's burgesses stuck to established usage and chose their mayoral candidates ready for the abbot's selection. The end of the story was briefly recorded in the Corporation Diary. Election of the three was done on 19 September 1539, but before that date

"the monastery there was suppressed and the abbot deprived of his abbey. And after this suppression all things remain in the hand of the lord king"

and this brief obituary marks the end of the story of four centuries of relationship between town and living abbey.

In most ways that relationship had been of mutual advantage, for the abbey brought employment, trade and visitors to the town, and the town gave the abbey prestige, services and income. At times historians have tried to read the relationship in terms of struggle, with each side striving to

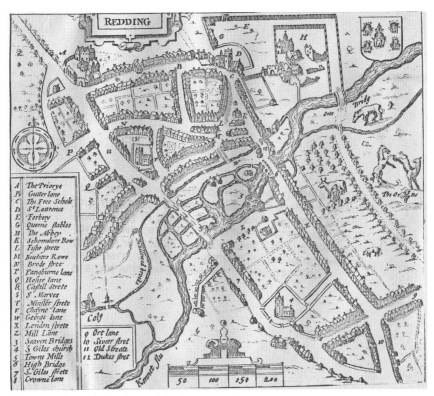

A | The Priorye
B | Gutter lane
C | The Free Schole
D | St Laurence
E | Ferbery
G | Queens stables
H | The Abbey
K | Schomakers Row
L | Fishe strete
M | Buchers Rowe
N | Bride street
P | Panaburne lane
Q | Holier lane
R | Castell strete
S | St Maryes
T | Minster strete
V | Cheyne lane
W | George lane
X | Lendon strete
Z | Mill Lane
3 | Seaven Bridges
4 | S Giles church
5 | Towne Mills
6 | High Bridge
7 | S Giles strete
8 | Crowne lane
9 | Ort lane
10 | Siuer stret
11 | Old Streate
12 | Dukes stret

Speed's Map of Reading, 1610

This, the earliest map of Reading, gives a good impression of the territorial relationship of town and abbey in the early 17th century, and, in fact, for the two or three centuries before that. Comparison with later maps shows that the abbey buildings here, with the exception of the inner gateway, are not accurately placed or represented.

make major gains from the other. In fact, what emerges is conservatism, the desire of both sides for most of the time to maintain agreements and practices, and only in times of tension do claims escalate. There are hints that the comparatively few serious disputes were exacerbated, or even caused, by personality clashes rather than by conflict of principles. Those of Reading's more important men, who desired to exercise the power that came with public service, were in no way cramped by the abbot, and could find ample scope in borough administration, through gild or abbey, in parliamentary representation and in part-time royal administration; and if some desired to gain more power, others were doubtless only too pleased to concentrate on their own activities and be spared more than minimal public duties in the town.

All major conflicts seem to have been between the abbot and a small, upper group of townsmen, the fifty or so burgesses of the gild merchant, and to have been sorted out in law or by arbitration, as between two increasingly equal parties. Reading had been a borough for many years before it was given to the abbot, and it was only as an attempt to score a legal point that he denied this; nor did he ever attempt to exercise the strict economic controls found in some other monastic boroughs. The great majority of the population had no say in the running of the town, and would have had no more say had there not been an abbey, and to many of them the abbey brought practical and spiritual benefits. Reading's relationship with the abbey doubtless reflected a common pattern: a few positively liked it, a few wanted change, the majority were essentially indifferent. Indeed, the majority possibly preferred the abbot's authority to being directly under that of a select group of burgesses who already, as employers, held the economic power. It mattered nothing to the lower classes whether abbot or burgesses owned the stocks; they were the ones put in them.

III

The Abbey in Royal Hands: 1539–1661

In 1539, on the 14th of November, most of Reading's inhabitants must have been present at the public execution of Hugh Cook Faringdon, Reading Abbey's last abbot. He had been tried and condemned for high treason, the accusation being that he denied that the king was supreme head of the English church. The trial had been held in Reading and the execution by drawing, hanging and quartering of the abbot and two clerics probably took place in the Forbury, and it was by far the most dramatic event in living memory or in the town's tradition but even before the abbot had been tried and condemned, royal agents had descended on the abbey. In September a local man, Sir Thomas Vachell of Coley, had been associated with one of the chief servants of Thomas Cromwell, Henry VIII's all-powerful minister, in making an inventory of the abbey's goods, and on the 17th of September many of its treasures – jewels from shrines, gold and silver objects, vestments – were despatched to the king. In the same month, or soon after, the abbey was emptied of its monks and lay servants were dismissed. In 1536 the abbot had attempted to minimise threats to his abbey by appointing Cromwell steward of the abbey for life, but to no avail, and with the abbot's fall Cromwell received a new appointment, that of High Steward of the borough. Thus it came about that the burgesses necessarily and wisely sought his permission to choose their mayor. They chose Richard Justice, one of the three previously nominated, and on 9 October Vachell, as deputy High Steward – he became overseer of abbey property and bailiff of Reading early in 1540 – administered the oath of office to him. Vachell continued his successful career, for he and an outsider, Sir William Penyson, were put in charge of the abbey, Vachell concentrating on its surviving portable wealth, Penyson on its buildings. The king appointed Penyson Chief Steward of the borough on Cromwell's fall and he and Vachell together, in 1540, in what was described as "the great hall of the late abbey", followed the old procedure where they selected the mayor from three candidates put forward by the burgesses; they then jointly administered the oath. In 1541 Vachell alone selected the mayor. Thereafter, by the terms of Henry VIII's charter to the town, the burgesses themselves chose their mayor, this being the first time, certainly since 1121, that they had had free and lawful choice of their own chief officer: and so it was to continue.

So all the abbey property, including the main site at Reading, came into the king's hand. The king could utilise high quality buildings at so convenient a distance from London, so royal accommodation was set up, concentrated on the former abbot's lodging – it continued to draw its water from Conduit Close in Whitley – with Penyson in charge as "keeper of the mansion house or chief mansion of Reading"; and stables for the royal horses were established in the dormitory of the former guesthouse. Henry VIII paid a brief visit and more formal visits were paid by his successors, Edward VI and Mary with her husband, Philip. Even if used only occasionally, the royal accommodation had to be kept ready, and the royal stables were in permanent use, so there must have been a number of people legitimately on the abbey site. There was also life on the fringe of the area, for the free school, revived or started by Henry VII, had become established in the refectory of the former guesthouse somewhere around 1486, and at some stage the abbey mill was turned over to commercial production. There must also have been servants of Vachel and Penyson keeping an eye on things and possibly carrying out some unrecorded stripping of fittings and small demolitions. However, as far as the townsfolk were concerned, it was basically a matter of one lord replacing another, and an ungenerous lord the king proved to be. The disappearance of the abbey had left a gap in the running of the town, which Henry VIII's charter attempted in part to fill by putting new responsibilities on the borough authorities. However, he gave no resources to cover new responsibilities, and all they received were the nave and side aisles of the church of the dissolved house of the Grey Friars as a new Town Hall. It must have riled Reading's burgesses to see how well rewarded – basically at the town's expense – were those who had helped carry out the royal plans. Penyson was granted the profits of the two fairs held in "le utter courte in Reading called le Forbury", Vachell was granted properties in the town and William Grey, of London, the predecessor of the Blagraves, was treated even more generously.

However, the death of Henry VIII in 1547 removed what later events showed to have been a restraining hand. His successor, Edward VI, was a minor and during the first part of his reign the leading man in England was his uncle, Edward Seymour, Earl of Hertford and Duke of Somerset, a grasping and rapacious individual. In July 1548 he received various grants including the Manor and Lordship of Reading and profits from the two fairs. He stayed, or planned to stay, in the royal accommodation in the abbey, and it is probable that Duke Street was formally or popularly named after him. In September 1548 he received an estimate that there were about 450 tons of lead on the abbey roof, a very worthwhile quantity, for lead had a great variety of uses. The subsequent operations may or may not have been approved by the Privy Council, but lack of such approval would be no deterrent, and this royal resource was blatantly carved up between Somerset and a leading official concerned with the disposal of monastic property, Sir Richard Sackville, Chancellor of the Court of Augmentations. The operation was primarily for the lead, and it was, appropriately, directed by George Hynde, a minor official and a plumber (i.e. a lead-worker) by trade, but during the three months it took, other material remains were dealt with, probably what remained from earlier, unrecorded, activities by Vachell and Penyson.

Hynde kept careful accounts of the material that passed through his hands, so this major episode in the destruction of the abbey is, fortunately, reasonably documented. The roofs were divided between the duke and Sir Richard, the former having those of the church, chancel, dorter and infirmary, the latter those of the north and south sides of the choir, the chapter house and the lady chapel. These were certainly stripped of their lead; some of the other roofs sold – library, prior's hall, "an old chapel", "the spire steeple roof", etc. – may have been tiled, but whatever the roofing material, once it was removed, decay soon followed. About 200 tons of stone were sold at 1s. 4d. (c.6p) a ton, not a great quantity, but its locations are interesting: for example, "upon two sides of the cloister"; "fallen down on two sides of the cloister"; "images and stones standing at the high altar"; "stone of the battlements (of the church) broken in taking down the roof"; "2 pillars of stone in the old chapel". In addition, eight houses were sold complete, including "the old lodging behind the infirmary"; "the jakes house"; "a little house by the waterside"; and another there "called a slaughter house"; "an old lodging (chamber) hall"; "a little lodging"; all going for between £1.13s. 4d. (£1.66) and £10. Woodwork taken included "the frame the organs stood on"; "an old organ case"; "cells in the dorter"; "monks stalls in the choir"; "a dais of wainscot", sold for just over £14. Over 13,000 each of paving and roof tiles went, some hundred-weights of copper, brass and iron, "the plaster of paris that went about the choir", 300 "old lathe boards", and glass, whole or broken. The oddments disposed of hint at a clearing out: "3 old bedsteads, an old table, 3 forms and an old portal" and 28 gravestones. So by mid 1549 most buildings stood gutted and roofless, their windows devoid of glass, building materials lying around the site and the cloisters, where lead was recast for shipment to London, largely in ruins. It was only fitting that charges brought against Somerset should include that of converting "lead, stone and stuff" of Reading Abbey to his own use. His connection with Reading ended with his execution in January 1552 and the abbey reverted to the crown.

The effect of all this on Reading can only be surmised. Emotional reaction among its inhabitants must have varied greatly, from tension and shock for the many to rejoicing for the few; for all there was uncertainty over the future and for some a pondering on what they could extract, honestly or otherwise, from the situation. Talk over all these happenings must have been endless, but those disapproving would have been wise to keep their opinions to themselves, for spies and informers were everywhere, and penalties, financial and physical, could be swift and unpleasant. No doubt many Reading folk wandered into the great abbey church, now empty, desecrated and stripped of its treasures. For all it would have been an emotional experience and many would deplore the loss of the relics. The burgesses may initially have regretted the removal of the abbot's authority, for in a petition to Cromwell they remarked that Vachell was not their friend and that they had little confidence in him and "ask that they may not be in such subjection under a bailiff", a difficult situation for he was MP for Reading from 1529 to 1547. Also there were more mundane reasons for regret, for economically the town went through a bad patch, though how far this can be attributed to the passing of the abbey is not clear. Obviously a major provider of poor relief had gone, likewise employment for abbey servants and craftsmen and pilgrims requiring services from the town. On the other hand, pilgrimage had become much less; much of the guesthouse had been diverted to other uses, the abbey almshouse for worthy widows had long since closed down, and the town now made its own provision for the aged poor; employment had been reduced, but there were at least some new jobs in the royal residence and stables. The Corporation fell temporarily on hard times, borrowing money and reducing the mayor's salary, but the galloping inflation that occurred in the middle years of Tudor England together with the Corporation's lack of resources had much to do with this. However, it is likely that some Reading folk took advantage of the situation. In 1538 the house and church of the Grey friars was dissolved, and soon after plundered by the mob. The abbey did not suffer in the same way, although petty theft of wood and stone would not be recorded. Payments made during the 1549 operations are very suggestive as they included "for watching the King's lead and timber from stealing and embezzling at nights".

One local organisation that benefited from Somerset's activities at the abbey was St. Mary's church, whose officials bought abbey material for the restoration of their church. Some specific items are detailed, such as the monks' stalls in the abbey choir, purchased for 53s. 4d. (£2.66), cost 10s. 6d. (52p) to take down and carry to St. Mary's in twenty one loads; also the chapel roof, pillars and "a little house" all of which occur in Hynde's accounts. Also purchased was "the door that stood in the cloister" and at least ten loads of abbey stone, twenty three of timber and six of tiles. Possibly a lot more abbey material was used in St. Mary's rebuilding, for the churchwarden's accounts do not always mention the provenance of the materials purchased. Of other Reading churches the needs of St. Lawrence's were very modest: in 1540 the churchwardens paid 8d. "for carrying the desks out of the abbey church", and there is no record of St. Giles's making any acquisitions.

The abbey, as we have seen, reverted to the crown on Somerset's fall and execution and in the same year, 1552, King Edward VI made a formal, and expensive, visit to Reading being escorted by the mayor "thorough the towne into the Kynges place", i.e. royal accommodation in the abbey. In

1554 Queen Mary and her husband Philip of Spain visited and stayed, although the ruined abbey must have been a sad sight for catholic Mary. She retained the abbey in crown possession and appointed the catholic Sir Francis Englefield, who also received extensive power within the borough, as its keeper. This doubtless checked unofficial destruction but there was deliberate destruction in the provision of abbey stone for the erecting of the Poor Knights' Lodgings at Windsor Castle. Activity included "masons choosing stones there", "masons taking down the great stones of the doors and windows of the Lady Chapel", "labourers digging stones out of the walls there", "labourers digging Caen stones out of the windows for the battlements of the new lodgings". Such activity could well account for the disappearance of the Lady Chapel. In 1556 a slight rearrangement of land took place in the Forbury. Previously parishioners of St. Lawrence's had been buried outside the north wall of the abbey church, but now the church was given a small adjoining piece of the Forbury as its churchyard.

In November 1558 the protestant Elizabeth I succeeded to the throne. Sir Francis Englefield chose voluntary exile in Spain and the abbey came once more directly under the crown. However, this occasion was significantly different because, for the first time, the town received a worth-while share of former Abbey property. Within two years of her accession, Elizabeth, on 23 September 1560, granted the town a splendid charter that in its sixty two clauses covered every aspect of town government in very favourable terms. A very important grant was to the Mayor, and Burgesses and their successors of "all that free and annual rent" from well over three hundred properties in the town, in addition to the rent from Englefield's considerable property there, which removed financial pressure from the town authorities. There were also grants which, although comparatively small, were the first received by the Corporation on the main site of the abbey. The refectory of the abbey guesthouse already housed the school and, as "la Scholehouse" had been granted by King Henry VIII to the then schoolmaster, Leonard Cox. However now the charter granted to the mayor and burgesses "all that our house tenement or messuage with the appurtenances called the Scholehouse in Redinge aforesaid", although they were now made responsible for the master's "salary and stipend" of £10 a year. In 1578 the Corporation emphasized its involvement in the area by transferring the Town Hall there from the nave of the former Greyfriars church, a place which must have seemed to a new generation of burgesses very unsatisfactory, and either now or later an additional floor was inserted in the refectory to make an upper chamber for use as a town hall, a lower one as the school room.

Also granted was property by the abbey's north gate, later known as the Hole in the Wall; the Compter Gate by St. Lawrence's church, in part of which a borough prison, the Counter, was established, the rest becoming residential – in 1584, for example, the schoolmaster paid rent for "a chamber in the gate leading to the churchyard"; and various small properties, such as "the two tenements over against the cage". Other property in this area was rented from the Blagrave family, which had begun its infiltration into the former abbey by buying up a crown lease in this area. The property rented consisted of a house and garden for the schoolmaster and an adjoining alleyway, 510 feet by 8 ft. 9 ins. This area on the west side of the Forbury also contained St. Lawrence's vicarage, a house and a couple of gardens, so it was well occupied, but the Corporation, by ownership or lease, had the largest share, but possibly the most valuable item in the charter involved the grant of four fairs. Two had existed from abbey times, their profits since going to royal supporters, but two were new, one in February, the other in September, each fair lasting three days. All these fairs were "to be holden and kept yearly in a certain place there called the Forbury within the limits of the same Borough or in any other convenient place in the said Borough". Rarely thereafter were they to be held other than in the Forbury. It would be very interesting to know how this specifying of a place got into the charter, whether, in fact, the Corporation asked for it. However it happened, Reading's Corporation, and through them the townsfolk, had for the first time some entry to and some rights over the Forbury.

Other Corporation requirements were more destructive. The crown had inherited from the abbot responsibility for Reading's 19 bridges, which were "very ruinous falling and in great decay for default of repairs and amendments". The charter transferred responsibility for them to the borough authorities, the queen discharging her liabilities by a grant of building materials. The mayor and burgesses were authorized to cut down and carry away 50 "timber oaks" from Whitley and Binfield and

"to dig take and carry away two hundred loads of stones called Ragged or free Stones in the aforesaid late monastery of Reading"

They were also permitted to

"pull down, carry and take away 2 cottages or sheds in the grange of the said late monastery and the timber and tiles of the same"

and similarly treated was "a house greatly ruined near the abbey mill". Possibly some better stone was taken now or later to roof over Holy Brook on the west side of Bridge Street. A further request, in 1577, for stone for repairs may not have been successful, and by the charters of Charles I and James II permission to levy tolls for bridge repairs was granted, not materials.

The town authorities can have had little trouble in collecting their stones, for by the beginning of Elizabeth's reign much of the abbey was in decay. A lease for 21 years, later renewed, gave Richard Okeham "the site of the monastery and capital messuage" with certain buildings there; all lead, timber, glass, iron, tiles and the like were to be maintained or disposed of for the use of the crown; and the lessee was to withdraw from the premises whenever the queen came. The yearly rent was £10 "in consideration that the premises are ruinous and have hitherto been of no value to the crown". The royal accommodation and its surroundings in the abbey must thereafter have been kept reasonably prepared against the various visits made by Queen Elizabeth I. Certainly Okeham's lease, from 1570, included an undertaking to repair without fee all buildings there "so long as the crown will provide the necessary materials". Likewise they must have been kept in some degree prepared during the reign of her successor, James I, although he never visited. Indeed, he gave the site to his queen, Anne of Denmark, who probably drew some income from it, for she had extravagant tastes.

However, a royal presence was maintained by the continuance, still in the old dormitory of the guesthouse, of the royal stables there, one of five such major establishments. Payment for looking after those at Reading continued unchanged up to the Civil War period at £6 20d. for custody, and the same for "cleaning and carrying away the soil". The site formed a self-contained complex. Some fields and parishes around Reading had to deliver hay for the royal horses to the barn, presumably on the site, and other features were the keeper's lodgings, called 'the Almery', the old stables and the new, the 'pondhest' to the south and the stable yard, with a gate separating it from the town. Maybe the stables explain the work of the two labourers who, in 1607, toiled four days apiece at the Corporation's expense in shovelling the dung-heap in the Forbury. Charles I visited early in his reign, in 1625, but only because of the plague in London. Various government departments came with him and many of these "were holden and kept in the great hall and other places of the decayed monastery of Reading", showing that certain parts of the abbey were still usable, although the Courts of the Exchequer and of Augmentations were established respectively in the Town Hall and the School House, where accommodation was thus removed from its normal use for some weeks.

This school and Town Hall was, as we have seen, the main former abbey building in the Corporation's control and as a much-used building it required regular maintenance, mainly glazing, especially as the assizes were held in it. Much glazing was done in 1607, the year that men had to be paid "for breaking the ice at the bridges in the great frost". New fittings included "a seat for the scholemaster" and some shelving. Possibly the school had a stone floor, for in 1606 a load of "pibbles" and their carriage cost 3s. 6d. (c17p). The only known new building occurred in 1608 when 38s. 11d. (c£1.90) was paid "for making a convenyant place for the skolers of the free skole to make water at", the materials for which included the modest total of 1,470 bricks: its cleaning in 1621 – "to the clensers of the scollers waull" – cost 2s. (10p). Sanitary arrangements for the school also figured in a lease for the Hole in the Wall in 1637, when it was leased to Sir Francis Knollys, described as "of Reading Abbey". The mayor and burgesses reserved to themselves the power "to erect, build and maintain for the use of the scholars of the free school of Reading a house of office in over and upon the west end of the ditch and banks of the said garden plot", and Sir Francis promised freedom of way. Whether it was ever built is not known, but the clause remained in every lease into the nineteenth century. At the other end of the site, the former abbey mill was working commercially: in 1627 the king was petitioned by the lessees against people setting up horsemills in the town for their own private use.

However, tension between king and Parliament was steadily increasing and Reading folk were willy nilly involved in the struggle. The period of the Civil War, 1642–5, when Reading was besieged, was the second of the

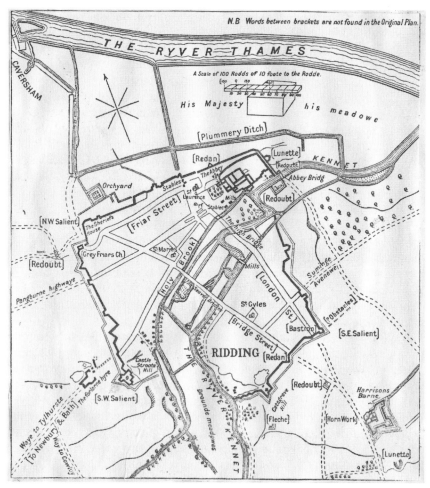

Siege of Reading, 1643
Based on a map in the Bodleian Library. It seems to have been drawn before the 'great ditch' was dug across the Cloisters and Forbury.

periods that saw concentrated damage to the abbey. In October 1642 a small, untrained Parliamentary force briefly occupied the town, but disappeared rapidly towards London in the face of Royalist advance. The king appointed the greedy and bullying Sir Arthur Aston as the town's governor, and it was probably for the royal visit in November that the Corporation paid labourers the considerable sum of 34s. (£1.70) for "cleansing the abbey" and "cleansing the way to the abbey". Sir Arthur carried out the king's desire that the town be fortified, and as part of this a great defensive ditch, with its rampart, was dug across the cloisters and nave, terminating in a defensive mound in the Forbury, the general aim here being to cut off the spur of higher ground on which the abbey stood from meadow and river. The inhabitants of the town were ordered to join in the work which, to give a clear field of fire for the defenders, must have resulted in much destruction of standing features in the nave and cloisters.

Matters drifted on unpleasantly for Reading's inhabitants, especially in January 1643 when Parliamentary artillery fired on the town. The real crunch occurred, however between the 15th and 25th of April, when Reading was besieged by Parliamentary forces under the Earl of Essex. He attacked from the south and west, causing considerable damage, especially as he had two of the heaviest guns from the Tower of London; and on the 19th of April Aston was badly injured by a tile, dislodged by gunfire, falling on his head. Soon after, another Parliamentary army under Lord Grey appeared on the north and east, setting up an artillery battery near the Thames against the defences in the abbey. This force also attacked, and on 25 April the Royalists surrendered. How the abbey fared in this is not known in detail. Possibly it was the main point of attack, and cannon balls could cause destruction, even if limited, for although its massive walls could resist seventeenth-century cannon, surface decoration and fragile features could not. The Plummery Wall suffered by having embrasures for cannon made in it, and the holes were still visible many years later.

Parliament's forces thus reoccupied the town; but in September 1643, after the first battle of Newbury, Essex and the Reading garrison of Parliamentary troops withdrew to London, and the town was reoccupied by the Royalists, who refurbished the fortifications. Then on 14 May 1644 Charles I again visited and decided to abandon the town, ordering that the defences be slighted (demolished). Next day, it was reported that "we are slighting the works here with all speed", and the fact that £200 was allowed for this suggests it was a considerable operation. It was either now, or possibly in 1642, that the east end of the abbey church suffered major damage. It was noted in 1779 that destruction in the crossing area of the church was consistent "with a mine having been sprung" and later archaeological excavation at the east end showed massive foundations shattered and tipped. Reading was reoccupied by Parliamentary forces, who failed to stop Royalists from Oxford kidnapping the mayor. Royalist slighting of the defences had been effective, for in July the Parliamentary commander

> "found the town so full of inlets and avenues that it is almost impossible to make it tenable unless it is fortified round as formerly . . . In the meantime we intend to fortify the abbey and to make two forts . . ."

Possibly destruction was not great and it was certainly lucky that there was no Royalist attack, for by late September the soldiers working on the defences refused to do more without pay. Not that they could have done much, for their commander requested "that we may have a supply of spades, shovels and pick axes, those we have being almost all broken". Advice on fortifying the town was given by Mr. Jacob Culemburg (Kuilenburg), chief engineer of Parliament's forces; but his recommendation to erect two small forts was, fortunately for the ruins, not followed. After this Parliament garrisoned the town properly, refortified it and, temporarily, used the school as an ammunition magazine.

Parliament took over all royal property on the king's fall and this included Reading Abbey, of which a survey was made in 1650. Standing, and in use as a barn, was the former abbey stable block by Holy Brook, with its yard and garden; likewise the mill, described as a granary. The "porter's lodge by the west gate", near St. Lawrence's church, provided the generous accommodation of cellar, hall, buttery, three chambers and three garrets, with a small yard and garden. The former royal residence was now in the occupation of Mr. Richard Knollys, and consisted of a considerable group of buildings around the inner gate:

> "two cellars, two butteries, a hall, a parlour, a dining room, ten chambers, a garret with a large gallery and other small rooms, with two courtyards and a large gatehouse, with several rooms adjoining to the said house, and a small garden with an old small house built with stone"

which last was probably the Abbot's lodging. In addition there were stable, dove-house and small garden, in all two acres. Of the old guesthouse the dormitory, now partly the royal stables, still stood, although not mentioned in the survey; and the dining room, now the hall-cum-school, being Corporation property was likewise not mentioned. Leased out was the monastery garden, the "great garden" of 1 acre 3 roods*; the 3 roods "now lying waste by reason of the fortification"; and the infirmary garden with buildings, possibly the old infirmary. The property called Grange Wharf, of 1½ acres was let to John Blake, and the dwelling there, consisting of "two cellars, a kitchen and a hall, a parlour and three chambers" could be the former east gate. These buildings stood, but some 8½ acres were full of ruins.

> "There is on the east side of the said mansion house (i.e. the royal residence) a great old hall with a very large cellar under the said hall, arched, with some other decayed rooms between the said hall and the

* a rood was ¼ acre

View of the Abbey Ruins, 1721

It shows the Chapter House from the Cloisters with the Refectory on the right

mansion house, with the ruins of an old large chapel, a kitchen and several other rooms, fit to be demolished, the materials valued at £200"

This high value shows a very large quantity of derelict material involving most of the monastic building. The "great old hall" is the chapter house, the "very large cellar" being bricked up in Victorian times and relocated in later excavation. The "decayed rooms between" were those of the cellarer's range. The "kitchen and several other rooms" were the domestic buildings to the south. The "ruins of an old, large chapel" were those of the abbey church.

Much of the abbey was thus in a derelict state by the mid-seventeenth century, but the building housing the Town Hall and the school seems to have survived well, rather luckily in view of its use as an arsenal and powder magazine. This use does not seem to have involved structural alterations, and expenditure over the next few years was on routine maintenance, mainly glazing and cleaning. The Corporation had taken – possibly usurped – certain rights in this east side of the Forbury, and the 1650 Survey seemed to admit this . . .

"There is, belonging to the said abbey, one court walled round called by the name of the Forbury . . . in which the town doth yearly keep foure faires and doth now lye common, and through which there are severall waies, as passages, into and out of the king's mead, into the great barne, stable and lodgings there . . ."

The Corporation felt confident enough to stop private building in that area . . . It also aimed to protect its undefined liberties in the Forbury for when, in 1651, Colonel Hammond gave orders that "a gate and styles be set up" at the entrance to the Forbury, the mayor and burgesses agreed

"so as he do in no measure prejudice the liberties of the town in the said Forbury. For if he do the Town will endeavour to defend their liberties".

In 1652 the mayor was asked for assistance in levelling the defensive ditch in the Forbury "whereby the fairs may be kept and the inhabitants of the town enjoy their privilege as formerly". The Corporation resolved "that some effectual course be taken", and this may have led to effective action, for in 1653 it was resolved that the next cattle fair "to be kept within this borough on St. James' day next shall be kept in the Forbury and not elsewhere".

The year 1660, that of King Charles II's restoration, really marked the end of royal interest in the former abbey, for he never stayed, and in 1661 leased the site "in free and common socage" for a rent of 40s. a year to Sir Thomas Clarges, a courtier, in exchange for his surrendering to the king a

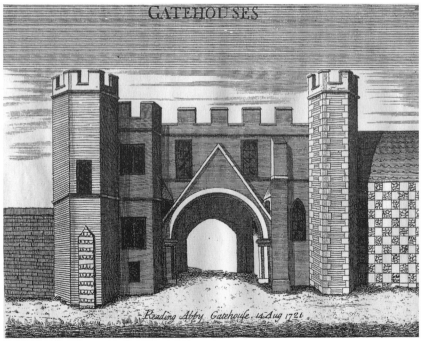

An idealized view of the Abbey Gateway, 1721

house in the Mews, in London. The royal stables in the abbey, however, continued in use, and in the next year the respectable sum of £517 19s. was spent on their repair, but trouble simmered for years. Five small houses had been built in the Forbury during the 1650's and these were subsequently required for the king's grooms and equerries. Sir Thomas considered the properties were included in his lease and, despite royal annoyance, he was proved right. To compensate him for giving up his claim, his lease was, in 1667, extended to 50 years and he received £160 back rent for the houses. But the £30 he received yearly thereafter for "the diverse houses for the use of the king's stables there" ceased after six years with no further mention of the royal stables.

The period since 1539 had certainly been a dramatic one for the abbey complex, but town and abbey had remained largely separate. However, by the end of this period royal interest in the abbey site had virtually disappeared, while the Corporation now owned former abbey property on the west side of the Forbury, including the old refectory of the guest-house, now a well-maintained building, housing school and hall. A further important gain had also been made, for the town authorities had established an apparently unchallenged customary right over at least part of the Forbury.

IV

A Time of Decline:
1661–late 18th century

❖ ❖ ❖

This period is one of the quietest in the history of the ruins, which virtually ceased to figure in national records. Doubtless material continued to be removed, but no records of this survive. Clarges appears to have shown little interest in the site, apart from the financial. Certainly any interest must have waned after 1684, for although he had won against the king, he appears to have backed down, before an irritated Corporation

> "Agreed that the major and company will assert their rights in keeping their fower faires throughout the Forbery, as it is graunted by their Charter, and that Sir Thomas Clarges be spoken with to remove all incroachments there, and that if he refuse soe to doe that then an action at law be brought against him"

This lack of interest culminated in 1723 when his grandson sold the lease to two local men, Anthony Blagrave and John Dalby. The Blagrave family, based on Southcote, already had a foot in the area as subtenants. Dalby was steward of the borough until 1760 when he was succeeded by his son, Thomas Septimus Dalby, who was given the freedom of the borough and acted as steward until 1779. But John Dalby had consistently borrowed money, using his share of the abbey as security, and after his death his widow and son sold it to Henry Vansittart, who in 1758 had been MP for Reading, for the considerable sum of £8,000. In 1780 the crown's lease to Blagrave and Vansittart was renewed for 21 years for a fine of £1,500 and an annual rent of £44 13s. 24½d (£44.66p), so undertenants inevitably had to pay increased rents. Henry and his second son were soon after drowned in the Bay of Bengal, but the family continued to hold its share of the abbey. Subletting and adaptation of buildings were bound to cause damage and the weather must have taken its toll, for Reading certainly had its share of gales, storms and hard winters. In 1754 General Conway, who had a good reputation for helping his local poor in bad weather, used "several massive pieces of wall which could not easily have been reduced", for building a bridge between Wargrave and Henley. In 1785 land at the east end of the abbey site by the infirmary and cemetery was purchased for a new House of Correction that in 1791 was enlarged and became the County Gaol "now placed so conspicuously among the ruins"; digging there in 1785 produced an unusual lead coffin that was sold to a plumber. Reading Corporation, of course, had no responsibility for the County Gaol. The abbey mill was noted as "still remaining and nearly entire", and continuing to work; the abbey gateway and adjoining house were, until 1796, occupied by a girls' school; and the chapter house survived nearly to roof level.

None of this, of course, was of more than passing concern to the Corporation, whose interests, apart from users' rights in the Forbury, were concentrated on the buildings and their immediate surroundings that formed a small group on its west side. A main visual change was the disappearance of an unknown length of the outer wall of the abbey at the Hole in the Wall, for by 1716 there were buildings "adjoining to and standing on the foundations of the said wall". The Counter and the old refectory containing school and Town Hall were in active use and needed constant attention. After 1700 cleaning costs were rarely itemized, but the earlier pattern presumably continued. In 1675–6, for example, Richard Cowdrey was paid

"for cleansing the rooms under the town hall and cleansing the garden and for a load of pibbles and a broome"

The removal of "two loads of soil and rubbish from the Town Hall and for bringing a load of pibbles" cost 3s., and "a new burch broom for sweeping up the dirt against the town hall" cost 2d. A labourer received 1s. for "shovelling and sweeping up the dirt near the town hall", and John Legatt the considerable sum of 4s. "for making clean the hall after the assizes". A little outdoor work was carried out, as in 1676–7, when Goody Legatt received 1s. 6d. "for twice weeding and cleansing the town hall yard", and in the same year snow had to be shovelled away. A very modest quantity of paving and gravelling was done, and at times the hall's two chimneys needed sweeping. It would be interesting to know what Smith the Scavenger transported in 1701–2 when he was paid 8d. "for carrying a load of rubbish from the hall". Rubbish was removed "from the town hall door" in 1742–3. Small items of maintenance, such as glazing, regularly occur, but at times larger works needed to be done. Externally, the walk adjoining St. Lawrence's church was, in 1680–1, repaired at considerable cost and carpentry was done on the town hall; in 1724–5 a stonemason received £9 15s. for work there and two years later a wainscot cost £4 16s. 4d. In 1740 it was ordered that the court at the north end of the hall "be altered and made more commodious" and in 1754 the hall got a new chimney. Internal decoration seems to have been whitewash, for an order to have it done, or redone, was made in 1753. In 1771–2 it underwent a major alteration after country gentlemen, involved in matters judicial, had complained. The Corporation agreed that the Council Chamber was "in a ruinous condition, the same to be pulled down" and action was taken. "Cash disbursed in building and furnishing the new Council Room at the Town Hall" amounted to £555 6s. 6d. with other bills being settled later.

The school received certain modest amenities, apart from the replacement of its bell rope: in 1734–5 a picture was acquired for £1 11s. 6d.; in 1740 bookshelves were to be made to shelve the books; and in 1770 the inscription over the doorway was to be "new done or repaired". Since the early eighteenth century, possibly earlier, rent was paid for "the town hall garden"; and at times the town hall water supply received special mention. In 1676–7 it cost 6d. to fill the "sinke" in the garden, and the same sum was paid the next year for "seven kilderkins of water used about the town hall". From the mid-eighteenth century a payment for water was made every two or three years or so, first to the appositely named Mr. Atwater, then to "the Proprietors", suggesting that the town hall was supplied from the waterworks in Mill Lane. The cost quadrupled to £2 1s. in some 30 years. However, the only suggestion of piped water occurs in 1761 when the watercock at the town hall needed repair.

Modest sums were recorded as spent on furnishings. "Mattes" were bought for 7s. 4½d. in 1703, for 13s. 6d. in 1712–13, and in 1728–9 "mending the matting in the hall" cost 17s. 6d. This seems distinct from the "carpitt" in the council chamber which,in 1704–6,was cleaned and mended at a cost of 7s., but there is no record of its being replaced even in 1723 when the chamber was refurnished with a new oval table and "'sufficient chairs", and £2 15s. was paid in 1725 "for mending pictures" there; they may again have figured among the pictures in the town hall that, in 1742,were "cleaned and beautified" at a cost of 9 guineas. In 1728 furniture for the hall cost the fair sum of £3 5s. In 1691 £17 was expended on tablecloths and napkins for the hall. Possibly it was not easy to keep the table linen, for it was speedily laid down that it should be kept in a trunk in the hall and "if any be left out or spoiled to be made good by the mayor"; however, by 1709 another 4 dozen napkins were required. Presumably existing table linen outlasted the old Town Hall, for by the time of the next big expenditure on such, 1786, the new building was in existence. Curtains are mentioned only in 1742–3, when they cost a mere £1 7s. 3d. In the same year evidence of feasts taking place there is supplied by the purchase of a dozen pewter dishes, six dozen pewter plates and as many saucepans as the chamberlain thought proper; and a decade later six "pannes" and a strainer ladle were acquired. That there is no mention of the purchase of glasses is a little surprising in view of the celebrations that at times took place in the hall: in December 1694, for example, the Corporation, gowned, met there "to drink their majesty's health in a glass of wine", the king having returned safely from Flanders; in 1726–7 "vitles and drink at the town hall" cost 13s. 9d., while in the next year wine alone cost 10s. 10d. and drink was doubtless available there in 1721, even if members had to bring their own, when 2s. 3d. was paid for "pipes and tobacco on the king's coronation".

So this former abbey building was, as the borough's civic centre, a busy place, encouraging much activity on this part of the abbey lands, although some activities were not especially desirable. In 1712 it was laid down that

> "no-one except aldermen or assistants are to dry their clothes in the hall, and anyone breaking a window by opening it is to amend it".

The problem was still there in 1723, when the sergeant was ordered

> "not to allow any persons whatsoever the liberty to dry cloathes in the Town Hall or bring netts to dry and mend in the hall without special leave from Mr. Mayor, but that the hall be kept clean and decent, and that the buckets belonging to the Town Hall be not made use of at assize time"

– the assizes marking an annual but depressing occasion there. In 1692 it was laid down that the hall was not to be lent "to any dancers or other to shew any sports or pastimes". In 1724 it was

> "ordered that no strolling players or puppet showers who travel the country to make shows or actings shall have the use of the Town Hall, and that this order shall be general to prevent sollicitations".

This prohibition was repeated in 1726 with the reason added

> "so that the mayor and aldermen may not seem to encourage such practices which tend to the corrupting of the youth of the said borough, and to prevent any damage which may thereby be done to the hall, the same having been lately beautified by the contribution of the neighbouring gentlemen and ladies".

At times security had to be looked to. In 1723 the keeper of the hall was ordered

> "not to entrust any person to come in or out at their pleasure, but the keys always to be kept in the custody of the . . . hall-keeper";

and the order in 1748, that new locks were to be put immediately on the lobby door, suggests some illicit activity. Towards the end of the century there seems to have been some slight easing of restrictions in the use of the hall when, in 1780, an application for the inhabitants (i.e. of Reading) to meet there was approved "providing the mayor's name is not made use of in any advertisement or handbill".

Movement outside the building could at times be impeded. In 1739, for example, it was ordered that "the ancient ways and passages to and from the kitchens and pantrys belonging to the Town Hall are laid open for the use of the mayor, aldermen and burgesses".

In the next year it was decreed

"that the little paved court together with the necessary house [lavatory] be separated from the passage where Mr. Hiley's boys go to and from school, it being thought necessary they should be open when the mayor's dinner is dressed",

elaborated a month or so later to allow the mayor to use the "said passage and necessary house" at feasts. Mr. Hiley, the schoolmaster, was allowed to use the passage between his house and the school, likewise the necessary house there "so long time as Mr. Hiley shall continue master of the said school". The lease of the passage cost him 5s. a year, but in 1761 the right to use it was very nearly lost to headmaster Spicer when Mr. Blagrave threatened to "shut up" the passage as the rent had not been paid. In 1780 a "convenient pavement" from the town hall to the church walk was ordered to be constructed.

The major act of destruction at this time to the abbey remains was not due to indifference, but to a revival of the civic spirit, although all improvements had to be brought in against a die-hard faction. The 1780s saw major changes in the borough, that included the statutory introduction of paving and street lighting and the rebuilding of High Bridge and among the most important of the changes was the building of a new Town Hall. The existing one had undergone considerable adaptations and repairs since its time as part of the abbey guesthouse. The floor of 1578, separating hall and school, had been replaced in 1672 when other work seems to have been done; and when the building was repaired between 1724 and 1727, work included replacement of the stairs and part of the floor, and cost the best part of £18; the schoolroom was then extended a little towards the north. At the same time, "the passage from the street to the stair foot was laid with broad stone, which before was paved with flints and pibbles". In 1781 repairs to the school were ordered. Earlier and later work, coupled with the major works of 1771, had greatly changed the building from its state in abbey times, certainly as far as its interior was concerned. Also the central columns that supported the pointed arches were most inconvenient. No voice in 1784 is recorded as seeking to preserve it on antiquarian grounds, and in a few months council opinion was strongly in favour of rebuilding rather than repairing. The new hall was in existence by 1786 and gained high praise, for "the present elegant room" was so much more satisfactory for the winter and race balls, and it had a "large and handsome" council chamber adjoining. It was built "on the ancient site" and arrangements were as previously set out with the schoolroom beneath the town hall. Unfortunately, the floor of the new hall was accoustically harder on those beneath. In 1789 parents complained that their boys "are sent home and neglected because they cannot be taught in the schoolroom", and Mr. (he became Dr. in 1792) Valpy, the headmaster, complained several times to the council that "the noises in the Hall prevent his teaching the boys in the schoolroom under it". A small committee visited, and "there experienced great inconvenience from the noises made in the Hall", and recommended that the Corporation should look out "for some other place for the schoolroom", but vague sympathy was as far as they went.

It is likely that the Headmaster's concern extended beyond noise to the actual safety of his pupils, for in 1793 Mr. Pilkington, the surveyor, listed two pages of defects in the buildings including the state of the pillars in the schoolroom. These were replaced, but nothing was done about the noise so, although for the time being a schoolroom continued here, a "large, commodious room" 52 feet long, was built nearby by Dr. Valpy at his own expense to replace it as the main schoolroom. The idea of a new schoolroom had been long in his mind for, in 1785, even before the new hall was built, he "having an intention to build a good room as a Hall for the use of the schoolmaster and boys" requested and was granted a strip two feet wide of the garden and scullery area of the old hall. This new schoolroom lay near the master's house, built earlier in the century. Before that, headmasters had occupied a house, part of the abbey gateway complex, somewhere near St. Lawrence's church but in 1731 the wealthy headmaster, Mr. Hiley, had built a house for himself and twenty boarders in the north of the Forbury near Vastern Lane on land just by the former royal stables and previously occupied by four tenants; and for this he paid rent to Anthony Blagrave. Mr. Hiley's daughter, Mary, married Anthony Addington "Doctor of physick", and he rented the house out to headmaster Spicer. It had been proposed in 1717 that a house be purchased for the headmaster, and in 1771 an unsuccessful attempt was made to buy the Hiley house for this purpose. However, in 1786 the plan succeeded, the house being purchased by subscription to be held in trust for the school by the Corporation. Dr. Valpy considerably improved the house, adding a hall, library and several more rooms. The Blagrave family held most of this former abbey area, and the land of both new schoolroom and headmaster's house was leased from them as was the surviving abbey building, the dormitory of the guest-house, subsequently, as we have seen, the royal stables. This building was dilapidated, but some of the school's boarders were accommodated there. In view of Blagrave predominance in the area, the Corporation was careful to define its own property:

"on taking down the old Town Hall it was ordered that 2 stones should be laid in the wall at the south end and level with the ground to ascertain the Corporation's land ... on both which stones is the following inscription viz. 'Corporation Ground see Diary 1785'".

Dr. Valpy co-operated with the Council in 1791 when it was somewhat wordily agreed

> "that a watercloset be made near the Town Hall under the inspection of the Chamberlain of the Hall Revenues, he receiving of the Rev. Mr. Valpy 7 guineas which he has agreed to give towards it, having had the liberty to remove a necessary house, which was a nuisance to him",

a small but significant improvement in amenities. In 1792 he had a successful brush with the Corporation when he refused to mend the schoolroom windows before the Hunt Ball as "he considered the schoolroom as his private property" and felt it was the responsibility of the Corporation if they wished the school to be used "at public times". The school also gave public performances of plays, frequently Shakespeare's as amended by Dr. Valpy, although in 1791 the play was Plautus's Aulularia when "after Act 3 Mr. Littlehales spoke a very beautiful elegaic poem upon the erection of a gaol on the ruins of Reading Abbey" – this being the year the new county gaol came into being. In the same year a piece of the Forbury was used to enlarge St. Lawrence's churchyard. For this the church authorities came to an agreement with Vansittart and Blagrave, the holders of the abbey site but, interestingly, the church obtained the consent of the Mayor and Corporation. Attempts by the school to earmark part of the Forbury as a playground were unsuccessful, as in 1776 when the attempt by Headmaster Spicer was thwarted by some of Reading's inhabitants, who asserted what they saw as their rights, by arranging a cricket match on the disputed grounds.

The Forbury figured at times in communal activities. In 1697 it was

> "ordered and agreed that the next St. Matthew Fair be kept at the west end of the Forbury from the path leading towards the King's Meadows for the selling of cheese and hops, St. Lawrence Church Walk for the servants and the Town Hall for the serges etc."

for this, the Cheese Fair, had outgrown Cheese Row (now the east end of Broad Street) and thereafter it was, like the other fairs, held in the Forbury. In 1785 the suggestion for another Cheese Fair involved admission of the real ownership of the Forbury, for application was made to John Blagrave and the executors of Henry Vansittart for their leave to hold a Cheese Fair in the Forbury annually on 21 March. It never took place, but rights in the Forbury were a touchy business, and maybe the Corporation was more circumspect than individuals had been in the past, for it had been individual townsmen who, in 1776, had successfully maintained against John Blagrave that youths of the town did not need to ask his favour to play in the Forbury. However, the main Cheese Fair, an ɔortant economic and social event, took place in September. In 1771 it was observed that "at our Cheese Fair was a prodigious quantity of cheese". It was likewise in 1785 when there was the largest quantity of cheese "that has been known for many years past", new cheese costing an average of £1 14s. a hundredweight, old cheese £2 2s. In 1791 the price of cheese "was very exorbitant", new averaging £2 3s. a hundredweight, old £2 17s. Actual quantities varied, but in a good year there could be 500 or more tons exhibited for sale; and at the July fair of 1772 was an especially large show of horses. Any of the fair days could attract undesirable elements. In 1790 pickpockets were very busy at the May Fair, and in the next year magistrates gave warning concerning large numbers of "idle and disorderly people" who would attend. They also warned about the pickpockets, sharpers and swindlers liable to attend the September Fair.

There were various houses in the Forbury. For example, the "celebrated" Mrs. Eades died in hers in 1745: she was a "person of great parts and judgment, excelling in teaching all curious works", who had for many years been mistress of the boarding school in Reading for young ladies, possibly that in the Forbury. Dr. Addington's maiden sister died in her house there in 1775; likewise Mrs. Knight "at an advanced age" in 1792. Mr. Elmes "who paints portraits in the best manner and of any size" worked at his house there. In September 1792

> "yesterday morning by the tempestuous weather the top of Mr. Simeon's summerhouse in the Forbury was torn off and carried some distance"

In 1786 Mr. Hawkes was allowed by the Corporation, for 1s. a year, to place "palisadoes" before his house that adjoined the Grammar School, possibly in the hope that a fence would keep its or other pupils out of his garden. In 1790

The Ruins from the west: Godfrey, 1773

The Ruins from the east: Page, 1786

> "the young ladies at Mrs. Tournelle's boarding school in the Forbury underwent a public examination in Geography . . . calculated at once to testify their proficiency, call out their attention and entertain the audience"

In the same year, Hamlet was performed in the schoolroom of the Grammar School, and in 1795 there was another public examination, this time of the pupils of Mr. Street's school in the Forbury, when "the young gentlemen performed with great credit to themselves". Mrs. Jesse also had a school and in 1794 she

> "presents her respectful compliments to her friends and will be happy in the honour of their company at her school house in the Forbury on Monday the 16th of October, being her public day for dancing, which will begin at 6 in the evening"

The exact site of most of these properties cannot be established, although Mr. Hawkes's house was in the west part and the Abbey School for girls was, until 1796 when it went bankrupt and left Reading, in the Abbey Gateway and adjoining premises. Jane Austen, the later novelist, had been a pupil there. One elegant eighteenth-century house, later known as 22 The Forbury, survived until the destructive 1950s.

The Forbury was used on many public occasions, for royal birthdays, coronation days and thanksgiving days were frequent. Three or four barrels of beer and wood for a bonfire was the usual provision for the general public, with wine for the Corporation. This last could be in generous provision, as in October 1697, when 3 dozen of claret and a dozen of canary were used "to drink prosperity to the peace, etc", and again in December when 1½ dozen of canary, 3½ dozen of claret and a dozen of white wine were needed for Thanksgiving Day. A similar quantity was provided in 1702, and in 1709 the chamberlain provided 3 dozen of claret, a dozen of white wine and 3 bottles of canary "to drink her Majesty's health on Thanksgiving Day". On this last occasion provision was made for 3 barrels of beer and 10s. for a bonfire in the Forbury, although beer and bonfire were at such times normally in the Market Place. Drink was rarely itemized thereafter, although in 1721–2 Mrs. Garroway was paid £4 2s. for wine on the king's birthday, and in 1728–9 "wine to the hall"cost a mere 10s.10d. As occasions for celebration continued, the necessary drink must have been privately provided. in 1772, on the king's birthday

> "at noon the 67th Regiment of Foot, quartered here was drawn up in the Forbury where they fired three volleys".

In 1789 there was an elaborate celebration to mark the king's recovery from illness: dinner for 283, starting at 3.30 p.m., was held in the Town Hall and,

> "on the mayor's announcing the toast 'God bless the king', a royal salute of 21 guns took place from cannon which were "planted on the hill in the Forbury . . . at 8 o'clock the whole company, preceded by the band of music, went in procession to the Forbury, where a display of fireworks was exhibited".

General topographical information regarding the Forbury is sparse. In 1755 the chamberlain was ordered to

> "pay Mr. Richard Simeon 5 guineas towards the expense of repairing the road through the Forbury and beautifying the other part thereof";

and in 1766 Francis Annesley was to be paid 10 guineas "for the improvements making in the Forbury". He had been concerned about Forbury Hill and had

> "more than once exerted himself in procuring subscriptions towards the repair of this delightful eminence".

However, by the late eighteenth century change was beginning to show in many aspects of national life, and although the full impact of these agricultural, industrial and intellectual changes was yet to come, matters were altering. Fresh ideas of civic responsibility were developing and there was a steadily increasing interest in antiquities and local history. In 1755 there was published "Forborough Hill in Reading, Berks, a poem", the first of many about that feature:

"From this delightful Mount what prospects rise
Demand our notice and create surprize,"

and it was clearly popular:

"Hither to this aspiring Hill repair
A crowd t'enjoy the soft salubrious air,"

and the Forbury was already a place of promenading, for

"Both sexes join the long desired walk,
And heighten friendship with instructive talk"

During the course of the eighteenth century a number of engravings of the abbey had been published, although many of these were idealized or inaccurate as, for example, was Stukeley's "North Gate of Reading Abbey" that appeared in 1721. The inner gateway, usually called the Abbey Gateway, was the favourite individual feature, and the second half of the eighteenth century produced a number of illustrations, such as those by Godfrey (1762), Rennoldson (c1770), Chesham and Sandby (c1770), Sandby and Rooker (1775), Hooper (1784), Robertson and Paden (1791). More extensive views of the ruins were produced, for example, in 1721, 1759 and 1775, and by Rennoldson (c1770) and Godfrey (1773). The most detailed set of engravings were the eight originally produced in 1791 by Tomkins for his book, "Views of Reading Abbey etc". on the abbey and the churches it held. The producers of these works were clearly aware that there was a public prepared to purchase them. Many engravings were published as books with accompanying texts which, with more or less philosophical brooding, described the state of the ruins, as on the lines of the 1755 poem:

"The rugged remnants tott'ring in suspense,
To curious minds a secret charm dispense"

Stukeley's brief, factual description of 1721 was not significantly bettered.
The year 1776, however, saw a major advance in writings on Reading Abbey for in that year was published a 6-page illustrated article in volume VI of the comparatively new journal, "*Archaeologia*", entitled "Observations on Reading Abbey", by Sir Francis Englefield, F.S.A. His ancestor had been keeper of the abbey under Queen Mary but had fled, as a catholic, on Elizabeth's accession (1558). Englefield viewed the abbey with the eye of a factual antiquarian, producing the first modern survey, accompanied by accurate plans and elevations. He noted its generally ruinous condition:

"The shattered and disjointed ruins of the buildings, which now remain,

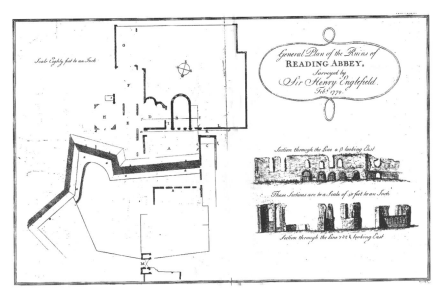

Englefields Plan and Sections

bear a character of majesty very singular and almost peculiar to themselves. Stript by destroyers of more than ordinary patience and industry, of almost every stone which cased the walls, they still, tho' built only of small flints, defy the injuries of time and weather, and have more the appearance of rocks than of the works of human hands . . ."

but his detailed information showed specific features to be better preserved. The abbey mills "still remain nearly entire, a very curious specimen of the magnificence of the rest of the building". The inner gateway also survived:

"The gate is of that semi-Saxon style which seems to prevail over most parts of the building with pointed windows and the arches of the gate round . . . Many persons now living remember its battlements".

The outer wall was "very inferior in strength to the rest of the ruins and is probably of a much later date", an observation confirmed, as far as the south wall was concerned, by later excavation on a limited length of its footings. The refectory, later represented by but a length of wall-core, had many features surviving. It was

"accessible now only through Mr. Clements house its door of entrance into the cloister being walled up. This room is 38 feet wide and at least 72 feet long, and has been highly ornamented with a row of intersecting arches, and above that a sort of arcade running round it . . . The whole upper end of the room bears its ancient stonework in the upper order" and he noted that the arches had been saved by being plastered up, adding, "it bears no marks of ever having been vaulted". The nearby cloister had "2 neat stone cupboards and between them a rough foundation", the former probably for towels, the latter the foundation of a stone basin for washing before meals. The north side of the cloister was visible, the whole of its west wall stood to a height of ten feet and had several doors in it "leading probably to smaller offices", and the cloister area with the rampart running through it "is now a garden", the "great hall and probably the chapter house" had, opening into the cloisters

> "three semi-circular arches with a window over each, and terminating to the east by a semi-circle with five large windows in it. The hall tho' 42 feet by 79 feet was vaulted with one semi-circular arch from wall to wall, apparently with stone ribs and at intervals filled up with a very curious substance . . ."

the "curious substance" was tufa, used for its lightness, and the extract shows that the large entrance had not yet been knocked out at its eastern end. Remains of a passage "two storeys high" to the north and the staircase to the south were still comparatively well preserved. The church, however, was in a very bad state:

> "Such has been the care taken to destroy it that nothing but a very diligent search could have led me to determine its site".

His "diligent search" obviously succeeded for he gives precise dimensions:

Englefield's 'two vast pieces of wall'.

"The dimensions of the church as deduced from these remains are as follows:

Eastern Chapel 102 feet long by 55 feet broad ⎫ These measures
Choir 98 feet long by 34 feet broad ⎬ are clear within
Side Aisles 19 feet broad ⎭ the walls
Transept 196 feet long by 56 feet broad
Nave probably 215 feet long

> "I say probably because the west end of the church is now entirely destroyed, and in its place a large and high rampart now crosses the whole ruin, through the Cloister Court, and ends in a sort of hornwork commanding the Thames and its meadow northward"

His overall figure for the "extreme length" of the church was 420 feet, its breadth 92 feet. He mentions one peculiar feature

> "There is a circumstance which is very singular in the walls of the church; that is, that the side aisles seem to have been separated from the rest by continued walls which are in some places 3 feet above the turf. This indeed I cannot account for . . ."

but which suggests post-dissolution building, reusing abbey material, and, as nothing more is heard of it, its subsequent demolition. He notes the "remains of a singular semi-circular bow" to the east of the cloisters, which he correctly identifies as "probably a chapel in the South Transept". Near the crossing of north transept and nave he observes that

> "a hollow remains in the earth where almost certainly a mine was sprung that reduced the church to an heap of ruins and pitched those two vast pieces of wall . . . into their present very surprising situation."

and the shattered foundations that later excavation has found in this area support his suggestion. He refers briefly to the cellar, filled in probably in Victorian times and since relocated with its reputed hole emptying into a "vault" that was probably a great drain and, in connection with vaults he observes that

> "persons who have dug in the ruins have . . . thought the chapter house to be vaulted (i.e. to have a vault or cellar) from the extreme hollow sound of the earth in digging. No opportunities have, however, offered to verify this".

He also included some true observations on building materials and methods.

His, then, is a sober, factual survey and the starting point for modern

Interior of the Chapter House 1797

studies, for hereafter the story of the ruins is reasonably well documented. However there is a little left unexplained, especially concerning these "persons who have dug in the ruins" and their purpose. Some of the digging of gravel and rubbish pits could well belong to this time, and the gardens in the cloisters were obviously dug, but was there any digging to investigate the ruins? If the church foundations were as concealed as Englefield reported, then, to get his precise measurements, he must have employed men to expose them, a primitive type of archaeological excavation, and if men were used here, why not elsewhere on the site: to solve, for example, the matter of a vault under the chapter house? Excavation was a favoured pursuit by gentlemen antiquaries and specialized labour was not then regarded as necessary but, whatever was done was on a small scale, and the ruins were not obviously affected. Nor do they seem to have been affected by any digging of foundations for new building; work in the gaol area showed how destructive this could be.

By c1790 this period of slow destruction, in contrast with the violent destruction of the preceding period, was drawing towards its close. Antiquarians might view and draw it, but no-one had a specific interest in preserving the abbey, no family had put roots down there and the site had been sublet into areas that were going their separate ways, indeed the area of the new gaol had already been hived off. What recognizably survived was what was in use, the mill, the compter gate by St. Lawrence's church, the inner gateway, and the dormitory and refectory parts of the old guest-house. The Corporation had established a *de facto* right to use the west part of the Forbury, and at fair time Corporation activity spilled over into

Abbey Gateway from the North
Tom Tomkins, 1797.

the east part where there were some private houses. All the Corporation actually owned of the former abbey buildings were the compter gate, the refectory of the guesthouse and, via the school, some vague rights in the dormitory of the guesthouse, the post-abbey royal stables. However continuing use did not make these buildings safe from destruction and, in fact, continuous maintenance and adaptation must have contributed to their decline. In 1785 porch and balcony were taken down from the compter gate and stocks and whipping post removed; the next year the compter prison went and its "necessary" was relocated; and, just before 1800, the compter gate itself was demolished. The new town hall had replaced the old, the former refectory of the guesthouse, in 1786, and the old abbey dormitory was decayed. In later times, these would have been listed buildings, but at the time any sentiment – not that there seems much locally – was attached to the core buildings of the abbey, not to these peripheral ones, and no conservationist voice was raised against their demolition. In this attitude and action, Reading's authorities seem neither before or behind public opinion but, as later happenings show, these events of the late eighteenth century virtually mark the end of the phase of deliberate destruction.

V

The Town and the Ruins:
late 18th century–1862

At the beginning of this period Reading produced three writers whose works were published early in the nineteenth century. They all used, and acknowledged, Englefield's work but added their own comments on the contemporary state of the abbey ruins. Charles Coates, in his scholarly work of 1802, was more concerned with the history of the abbey than with its current condition; but he commented on "the new (1793) county gaol placed so conspicuously among the ruins" and on the hardness of the abbey's foundations that were unearthed in building the prison. This latter point was taken up by Tomkins, for the ruins

> "though stripped by destroyers of more than ordinary patience and industry of almost every stone which cased the walls . . . defy the injuries of time and weather".

Tomkins was illustrator and engraver rather than historian, but he added interesting information concerning the inner gateway

> "The abbey gate is almost entire. . . There were battlements on the upper part, which were so decayed and dangerous to passengers that it was found necessary to pull them down some years ago, and several courses of brickwork were added, which appear so unpleasant to the eye and take off from the grandeur of the gate".

John Man's book was published in 1815 and in it he gave considerable space to the current state of the town, including that of the abbey. The site continued very untidy, for the abbey was

> "now reduced to a mass of ruins and involved in so much confusion by the broken fragments which have fallen in almost all direction"

that it was virtually impossible to trace the outline of its building. He concludes:

> "From the above imperfect sketch of the abbey and its precincts some

idea may be formed of the strength and extent of this once stupendous structure, whose ruins though still venerable from time, are fast mouldering away and will, probably, in a few years entirely disappear".

As the abbey was in private hands, there was no check on activities carried out there: temporary buildings were erected and the old adapted to various purposes. One of the most striking adaptations involved the chapter house in which, in 1812, a school for National Education was set up by subscription, £424 being subscribed, so

> "with this sum the committee erected two spacious rooms within the walls of the great hall in the abbey, sufficient to contain from 300 to 400 children; at the east end apartments are fitted up for the residence of the master and mistress; and however much antiquaries may regret this disfigurement of the finest and most perfect remains of this once beautiful abbey, it must be allowed that it could not have been employed to better purpose."

This may have been the occasion when an entrance was broken through its east wall and recesses made for ceiling timbers, and typical of piecemeal addition was the cottage built in the former North Transept. Digging in the ruins for gravel and building occurred, but any archaeological investigation seems to have been incidental. Tomkins, in 1805, referred to "several who have dug" in the chapter house, and Man mentioned "recent digging" there in connection with the National Schools. Coates wrote of finds unearthed when foundations for the new gaol were dug in 1793, and

> "in the same year some workmen digging by accident near the south transept found some fragments of glazed tiles; which being known they were requested to continue their search; at the depth of six or seven feet they discovered fragments of glazed tiles, part of the base of a clustered pillar and a piece of stone with zig-zag ornament of an elegant pattern".

The depth and finds would suggest that they dug where digging had already happened, which might help explain the author's view that "nothing of any consequence has been found among the ruins of the abbey". Man was more optimistic. He recorded the finding of a stone sarcophagus in 1815 by workmen digging for gravel in the nave of the abbey church, and opined that

> "if the interior of this ruin was carefully investigated there can be little doubt but many interesting discoveries might be made".

Over the next few years, matters continued much as ever. The owners seemed to have no objection to people wandering around or picking the wallflowers growing in the walls. Pieces of the ruins were liable to demolition; a branch road was made to the National Schools from the main road in the Forbury and some digging occurred. In March 1828 a macabre event took place when a scaffold was erected on the west side of the gaol for the public execution of Burnett, White and Field, who had killed a gamekeeper during a poaching foray. It was estimated that there were between 16,000 and 20,000 spectators, and

> "the venerable ruins of the once proud abbey of Reading were crowded with people".

The rising national concern over antiquities did not, in these years, perceptibly involve Reading Abbey and obvious sentiment was limited to a couple of second-rate poems. The sixteen stanzas of that of 1811 include

> "Here, as some say, Matilda's ashes sleep,
> And here entomb'd Henry the founder's head;
> Where now perchance some straggling kine or sheep
> Trample the ashes of the royal dead.
> "In many a cumb'rous heap like massy rocks,
> Disjointed, reft, the consecrated pile;
> The keen researches of conjecture mocks,
> While o'er its fate destructions daemons smile".

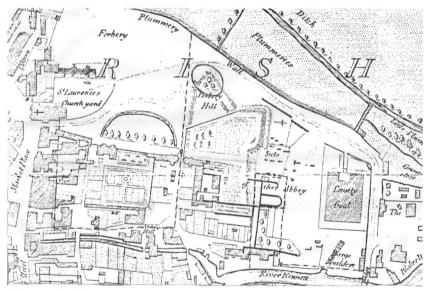

Plan of the Abbey c1802

And the other is a variation on the theme:

> "Unheeded the dust of the mighty reposes,
> Unmarbled, unknown the spot where it lies:
> No vestige the fabric in ruins discloses
> Of aught but the ravage of time as he flies"

although the main point of its six stanzas was the National Schools in the ruins. The abbey's decay could, as late as May 1831, be regarded as romantic:

> "The ruins of Reading's once magnificent abbey, 'defac'd by time and tott'ring in decay' add greatly to the variety of the scene, and contribute to render it to all a place of no ordinary interest."

But by no means all were prepared to watch it disappear, for when earlier in that year it had been announced that Mr. Vansittart planned to demolish his part of the ruins to construct a road and buildings, the *Berkshire Chronicle* did not pull its punches:

> "We are sure we are expressing the sentiments of the whole of the inhabitants of Reading in execrating an idea worthy of a Goth or a Vandal"

and a local poet joined in the fray:

> "Has fate decreed that yonder ancient piles
> Must be demolish'd by rude modern art,
> And on their site some ruddy bricks and tiles
> Rear a new dome for speculation's mart?"

The author, Mr. William Tyler, was among the first to back sentiment with cash when, in July, a subscription list was opened for purchasing the main part of the standing ruins. Earlier that month, following a "highly respectable meeting" in the council chamber, a strong committee, headed by the mayor, had been formed to negotiate with Mr. Vansittart and subsequently to raise the £500 he was asking for the site. The owner was very co-operative, even paying the conveyancing fee, and by September 1833 the half acre of the ruins formerly held by Lord Bexley (as the head of the Vansittart family had just become) was in the hands of trustees, secured for the use of the public and with the promise of no further dilapidations. At first the money had been raised comparatively quickly, £300 within two months, including a generous 10 guineas from the aged Dr. Valpy, but it took almost all the following year to raise the rest. However, there was little reason for the sarcasm of 1832 when, in a dispute over how to spend the money raised for the coronation celebrations, "unquestionably the best joke of all, some proposed applying the money to the purchase of the Abbey ruins from Mr. Vansittart".

Reasons for subscribing varied: civic pride, as commended by the *Bath Chronicle* and by the local paper; antiquarian interest, sentimentality, and a rising concern with public amenities

"The beauty of the situation and the picturesque disposition of the ruins would, if directed by the hand of taste, form a scene with which the most fastidious lover of nature might be delighted".

Matters inevitably moved slowly after the purchase, for after purchase and expenses of £505 only £5 remained to cover layout and upkeep, and even after an adjustment of accounts only £16 10s. 10d. remained. This shortage of funds was not generally known to subscribers who felt that a committee should be appointed to see to the laying-out of the grounds. In fact, the grounds remained completely fenced-in, and accessible only by trespass through neighbouring property. Unfair blame for the delay was put on the National Schools, still established in the chapter house, but feeling against them was partly their own fault. A subscriber queried their continuance there from

"observing the great injury done to the ornamental work, discovered during the investigations carried on by Mr. Hawkes, and which, I am afraid, must be attributed to the scholars of the National Schools".

But although they left the Forbury in 1835 and their "house" had been levelled with the ground by the end of 1837, there was no movement until January 1838 when at a meeting of the four available trustees it was merely resolved that they could proceed no further due to want of funds. But suggestions were made: that the subscription appeal be renewed and that the proprietors of adjoining land, the county of Berkshire – on the prison side – and Mr. Wheble should carry out their obligation of fencing their sides of the site, for enclosure as soon as possible was vital to prevent

"the encroachment of workmen employed in building speculations on neighbouring sites."

It was also pointed out that it would make an excellent place for the Reading Band to perform. What seems to have triggered off activity was permission being sought and granted for Reading Horticultural Society to hold its shows in the ruins, and possibly the Society itself tidied the grounds as well as producing the marquee; certainly the first show there on 23 May 1839 was a success, aided by "the beautiful ruins" and "the beautiful view" from them. clearly an improvement on the previous venue, the town hall. By June much work had been done due to the exertions of "one or two spirited individuals" and, soon after, a committee was in existence and subscriptions planned. The band's evening performance on 8 August attracted a large and appreciative audience, and at the end of that month

> "This admirable promenade continues to attract large attendances . . . and the grounds abounded with the beauty and fashion of the town".

So the first phase in the rescue of the abbey had been successfully, if modestly, accomplished; and although the town had not, as such, been involved in the purchase, these ruins were now, thanks to the work of comparatively few individuals, held by trustees on behalf of the townsfolk. It was a pity that no poet appreciated the significance of the occasion: "Lines written after visiting the Ruins of Reading Abbey" contained just generalized melancholy, as

> ". . . there stands the shattered
> Lonely pile, a thousand years surviving
> Time's spoil, and by his shadows darkened.
> Inhabited by wind, whose hollow moan Dies on the ruins. . ."

Although local sentiment could pride itself on this acquisition, it had made no perceptible effort to acquire the rest of the Vansittart holding in the ruins which consisted of over an acre extending south from the Abbey Gateway and including the cloisters and refectory. Here, by the end of 1832

> "The destruction of the houses standing on the site of the abbey has been nearly completed, and a considerable portion of the walls of the abbey have been demolished".

including the arches still standing at the end of the refectory. A suggestion that the area should be purchased as a site for a general cemetery was, fortunately, not realized. Who was responsible for the destruction is not clear, for Mr. Vansittart was actually negotiating the sale of the rest of his holding in the abbey – which included the east part of the Forbury – and by September 1834 had sold out to Mr. James Wheble of Woodley Lodge. Possibly Mr. Wheble had plans for excavating the cloister area, but he had done nothing about it by the time he died in 1840, and in 1843 his son, James Joseph Wheble, sold it, for £730, to a builder. It was soon sold on to John Weedon, a local solicitor, who in 1844 bought from Wheble a small strip on the west side of the site that included the east part of the Abbey Gateway. A new road, Abbot's Walk, was made, and over the next decade twelve superior houses were built with their back gardens extending well into the cloister area, their building involving destruction of footings and tiles in the south aisle of the church. This cloister area, sympathetically treated, could have shown off the ruins to great advantage, but the townsfolk never had a further opportunity to purchase, and in the 1930s the houses and gardens were acquired by Berkshire County Council as was St. Lawrence's Church School, built in 1852 on the west of the site. One scheme James Wheble certainly seems to have had in mind in purchasing the Vansittart holding, for by 1837 he had given land there, that included the area of the North Transept, was as a site for a catholic church. He also paid most of the building cost. It may have been his desire to have a building in keeping with the abbey that led the architect, Pugin, to design it in the "Norman" style. The church, dedicated to St. James, was finished just before the donor, in July 1840, suddenly died.

Over the next few years the ruins with which the town was concerned continued short of money for development. In February 1840 a fund-raising ball, under the patronage of the mayor, was held for band expenses and for general beautifying of the area. Reading folk were urged to give financial support and not to lose out to "towns of inferior resort" for more would leave the town than would visit it

> "as long as its present dull and inattractive character continues unaltered".

Routine basic maintenance characterized the following years, and it was not until 1854, when the town acquired part of the Forbury that the local Board of Health extended its concern to the ruins, putting them under the gardener in charge of developing the Forbury Pleasure Gardens. Possibly activity there was a little too horticultural. By February 1857

> "It is pleasing to observe that the grounds around the ruins of the once famous Reading Abbey are about to be put in such a state as to render them an agreeable place of public resort in the summer. Employment has been found there for the distressed workmen in cutting out paths and in forming gardens, and already considerable progress is made with the work. The object will be much promoted by any gentleman having superfluous plants and shrubs forwarding them to the gardener at the pleasure gardens, under whom the men are employed in the abbey ruins."

In the event, "some shrubs" were "promised by a few gentlemen" but, fortunately, Messrs. Sutton made "a very liberal contribution of trees and climbing plants" so it was soon "tastefully laid out and planted with shrubs." A further hopeful suggestion was that suitable timber be given for rustic seats to be placed in the ruins.

The first hint of linking the pleasure gardens and the ruins occurred in 1855, and by 1857 it could be expected that "a short, subterraneous communication with the Abbey Ruins will soon be effected". Negotiations continued and by the next year it could be firmly stated that "arrangements had been made by the trustees of the Roman Catholic chapel to give up to the Board (of Health) sufficient ground for the purpose of effecting a connection between the Forbury Gardens and the Abbey Ruins".

The work was completed by May 1859, and excavating it had resulted in the digging out of much abbey material, including flint and carved stone that was used in constructing the arch. The new approach

"with the banks necessitated in its construction has been converted into one of the most ornamental features of those highly appreciated places of public recreation".

and it was fitting that the thanks of the Board of Health were unanimously given to the Rev. J. Ringrose and to Mr. J.J. Wheble who had made the land available. About this time, a less happy approach was proposed: that an underground tunnel should run from the County Gaol and thence under the ruins of the Forbury to the new assize courts on the west of the abbey gateway. It was to be done at the County's expense but there were, understandably, objections and within weeks the project was shelved indefinitely.

This same year, 1859, saw the acquisition by the town of the last major part of the standing ruins. The area to the south of the chapter house had been in the hands of the late Richard Buncombe, timber merchant. Purchase by the town was first suggested in 1858. Its benefits were obvious, but there was a slight element of caution, for if it were acquired

"one superintendent would not be sufficient to keep the mischievous and badly-disposed in order, or check their practices".

In addition to the area between the chapter house and the river, the latter's north bank as far as Blake's Bridge was included in the sale price of £700. The late Mr. Buncombe's representatives offered £50 towards this, and the remainder of the purchase price was advanced by Mr. John Simonds. The town authorities, in their new zeal for acquiring amenities, would in the last resort have found the money, but it was still expected to be raised by public subscription. A dozen well-known firms and individuals promptly raised over £150 and all "desirous of prompting the improvement of the borough" were exhorted to subscribe as soon as possible, for

"There are few ruins which embrace so extensive a site or present such majestic and solemn grandeur as these when viewed from the point described (i.e. the south side of the chapter house). A movement in a monetary direction will secure this great ornament to the town, and be an even greater attraction to the stranger than this favourite spot already is".

A much advertised Grand Summer Fete was held in the Forbury and ruins on 11 July 1859 to raise money for the cause. The ground "was levelled and nicely gravelled throughout" and music, magic and fireworks were promised. But only half the anticipated number of visitors came and a measly £21 was all that the appeal fund gained: about the same time, the fund benefited by over £10 from a largely unadvertised Temperance Fete held there. In August the Board of Health planned to apply to "some gentlemen residing in the neighbourhood of the town" for subscriptions, and by the end of the month the grand total subscribed and promised was £370. This had risen to £500 by the end of the year, but with no real hope of more, and in 1860 when cottages at Abbey Walk were offered to the newly-established Improvement Committee by the Buncombe estate, the £250 required was found from resources. It was planned that one of these cottages should be occupied by the head gardener. Something had possibly been done about the open surface drain behind the cottages, that six years earlier "poisons the surrounding atmosphere", but they were currently described, in November 1859, as "the unsightly and insanitary buildings known as the Abbey Wall". The head gardener never took up occupation.

The town could take credit for its acquisition of the abbey when, in September 1859, the British Archaeological Association paid a prestigious visit to inspect Reading churches and the ruins, slightly spoilt as Mr. Pettigrew could not finish reading his paper on the History of Reading as the train was due to depart. Possibly it was fortunate that work in the new area did not start until after the visit, for the levelling there resulted in some rather cavalier treatment of its archaeology. As part of the operation, a terrace walk with chestnut trees was created between Blakes Bridge and Abbey Street, just outside the abbey precinct. By May 1860 turfing, gravelling and terracing had been completed, Mr. Davis, the head gardener, receiving much credit for the work, and Messrs. Sutton again made a generous gesture, supplying *gratis* £23 7s. 9d. worth of trees and shrubs for the new area. Work was completed in time for Reading Horticultural Society's Grand Floral Exhibition in May, that occupied the whole of the ruins with "a tent of immense size" in the new area. The very successful show was repeated in May 1861, with even greater success, and in May 1862

> "In a few hours those grey old ruins were lighted up with a splendour that far surpassed any feast day illuminations of earlier days. . . It was as if the old monastic remains had been endowed with new life".

Unfortunately not all were pleased. Among the most vocal of those dissatisfied was J.C. Buckler, an architect of national standing with a keen eye for antiquities, who over many years did a very competent survey of the ruins and wrote about them at some length. Much of his diatribe, condemning destruction old and new, had no bearing on the Corporation's activities. He commented that the "cold, money-getting population" of the present day did not appreciate the major antiquity in its midst for

> "the grand monument of Reading has never received any favours from the town"

which had always regarded it with "indifference or contempt", while greedy owners and "the idle and the vicious" continued to inflict damage. However, in his eyes, the ruins had fared no better in the hands of the Corporation for

> "The treatment which the ruins have endured since the abbey precinct was chosen as a site for a pleasure "garden has proved destructive in the extreme".

with walls destroyed or pierced to make way for footpaths, spaces and flower beds. In fact

> "it would be hard to find another instance of such callous barbarity as the present age has witnessed here".

but his voice was lost in the chorus of approval of the abbey as a pleasure ground rather than an archaeological and antiquarian site.

Certainly, as far as the archaeology of the site went, these years were not fruitful and there was no significant improvement on the situation portrayed in Coates and Man. The only excavation carried out for its own sake was that by Mr. James Wheble, FSA, who, since purchasing the property "has lost no opportunity of leisure for gratifying his taste and talents in exploring these antiquities". "these antiquities" being the abbey church. Work started in 1833 after later buildings there were removed, and in 1835 activity extended to the "north side at the choir end of the church" where some rather prosaic build-up was noted, but most attention was concentrated on a highly decorated carved stone found there. Expert opinion varied in dating it between the 10th and early 12th centuries, but people could judge for themselves, for a lithograph was published at an expensive 18d. It became the font for his new church. It is not clear how far Mr. Wheble realized his aims, for he desired to trace the walls and "this he has done by laying open the grounds at considerable expense". His activity recovered a "quantity of stone facings" that he proposed to incorporate into his new catholic church, the building of which caused some destruction in the north transept. Possibly Buckler used, unacknowledged, the results of this digging for his plan; if so, it is the only record that has survived. Earlier, in 1815, gravel digging, probably in the choir area, disclosed an elaborate broken stone sarcophagus; and there was some undefined activity by Mr. Hawkes in the chapter house. There was little recorded archeological activity in the area held on behalf of the townsfolk, although in 1838 a rumour, arousing indignation, circulated that

"Mr. Wheble has been empowered to remove the earth and rubbish from the interior of the ruins and appropriate any valuable architectural remains to his own use".

It was also stated that he was not even a subscriber! Some undefined excavations were carried out in the main group of ruins in 1842, when "a patterned glazed tile dated 1301" was found; and in the north-east of that area in 1857 in "the process of converting this interesting spot . . . the base of a very fine pillar" was located. Two years later, workmen landscaping just south of the refectory

"came upon an apartment about thirty feet square in which were found several finely carved stones".

A few archaeological finds were made incidentally in areas outside that held by the town. In 1841 a stone coffin came to light near the new catholic church "in the course of levelling the grounds", and another in the inner court of Reading gaol "in excavating mould to adapt the surface for gardening purposes"; while excavations on the west side there disclosed part of the foundation of "one of the semi-circular ends of a chapel" in an area where "portions of an old pavement" had at times been dug out. Foundation work for the new Assize Courts and Police Station between Forbury Green and Abbey Mill produced "subterranean walls and enclosures".. No doubt many smaller digging efforts or keen-eyed searching produced relics of the abbey and its times, such as the reported penny of Edward I or the abbey seal. Buckler was, as usual, unfavourable. "Mischievous industry" he considered "has brought small features to light only to exterminate them" and, generally,

"They dig in the earth with labour that they may exterminate the hidden foundations of once lofty and valuable buildings"

and he was especially angry over a wall discovered in the apsidal chapel of the south transept, as

"Before the writer could return to Reading to delineate the elevation of this valuable fragment the greater part was wantonly destroyed".

Two archaeologically-unfortunate episodes escaped his censure. In 1859 Mr. Myres, the contractor, excavated 30 cubic yards of stone from the area of the projected Assize Courts and Police Station, which the Forbury committee planned to purchase for £10 to repair the abbey gate, and in 1861 the surplus soil from the Forbury, with whatever it contained, was used for filling the Portman Brook ditches.

There was, at the end of this period, one large-scale excavation done partly for archaeological purposes, and many years after the event Mr. J.

Okey Taylor, who had played a major part in organizing it, gave a brief report. After purchase of the Buncombe property

> "about the same time . . . there was much distress in the town owing to exceptionally severe frost. A relief fund was raised . . . (and a large number of labouring men were employed in excavating the site of the Abbey Ruins. Under the supervision of a small committee . . . the excavation was continued largely at the cost of the Relief Fund and after at the public cost, so that the entire area of the site was excavated to a depth varying from two to five feet and the soil thus removed was conveyed to the river frontage and was chiefly the means of forming the embankment to Blake's Bridge".

He mentions the many pieces of carved stone found, some of which were used in the construction of the arch between gardens and ruins. He also mentions three column bases in the nave of the church and a tesselated pavement south of the refectory; and the finding of these widely separated features *in situ* supports the point of extensive excavation, but no other record is known to survive.

The remaining feature of major concern to the Corporation was the abbey gate, the inner gateway between Forbury and claustral area, and the best-surviving part of the abbey. At the coronation celebrations of 1821

> "the noble gateway was adorned with a large regal star"

and Buckler, obviously writing before its restoration, refers to

> "the magnificent gatehouse which in modern days has not been viewed with the regard it deserves".

It had lost its dangerous battlements many years before and had gained some unsightly brickwork, but it was certainly the most illustrated feature of the abbey. In 1840, for example, was advertised:

> "a small view of the Abbey Gateway exquisitely engraved on wood, is just published on superfine letter paper at 1d. per sheet".

However, by 1854 it was "manifesting the fatal encroachments of time", with a bulging buttress and enlarging fissures. Understandably no repairs were done in the next few years, for its west side was included in the Blagrave property in process of being sold to the Corporation. Negotiations lasted from 1857 to 1860, but by 1859 plans were firmly in hand to make this part of the gateway an office for the surveyor of the local Board of Health. The east side of the gate was formerly Wheble property that had been sold in 1844 to John Weedon, a local solicitor, and his widow now sold it to the Corporation for £50. The plan was to make this part a residence for the gardener, now called Superintendent, of the Pleasure Grounds: on the face of it, most undesirable as a residence, and even less attractive than the proposed cottage at Abbey Wall. In February 1859 the Board of Health optimistically announced that it would "shortly be undertaking the repairs and alterations of the Abbey Gateway", but quibbles over the cost and unsatisfactory tenders carried the matter through June and into August, when it was felt that Mr. Marshall, Surveyor and Inspector of Nuisances to the Board, was not the man to restore a medieval building: maybe justifiably, for

> "the construction in the Pleasure Gardens of a modern elliptical arch with old Norman materials proves him to be devoid of its spirit".

By 1860 the contrast between the new assize courts and "the ruinous state of the fine old Abbey Gateway" was painfully obvious, and

> "Our ancient Abbey Gateway is gradually yielding to the combination of time and tempest, whilst the Authorities are debating whether it is better to attempt the restoration or to quietly let it fall".

The cost of around £1,000, the estimate of George Gilbert Scott, the leading restorer of the day, was daunting. A suggested solution was that the Board of Health should pay £500 and a subscription list should be opened for the remainder. Alderman Blandy, a leading spokesman in favour of restoration, forcefully observed that

Collapse of the Abbey Gateway

"it materially detracted from the beauty of the front of the County Courts . . . it could not remain as it at present stood – it was a perfect eyesore".

Members of the Board very much agreed and, as individuals, quickly subscribed over £140; within a week almost half the sum, had been raised, and by the beginning of June subscriptions totalled £460. Gilbert Scott's report itemized a daunting list of works that needed to be done there, but he encouraged the Board by pointing out that

"the gateway is a work of architectural interest and value and is well deserving of the most careful restoration".

Inevitably an Abbey Gateway Committee was appointed with the equally inevitable appointment of Councillor J. Okey Taylor as its honorary secretary, and its first scheme was to lower the road under the arch by two feet. But by the end of August, Gilbert Scott's plans and specifications had been received, were available for public comment and praised in the local press:

"The designs are exceedingly elegant and when carried out the building will form one of the principal attractions of the town".

In September old doors and windows were opened up to let potential contractors see what was needed, and

"the clearing away of ruinous portions has opened up an ancient staircase by which access was gained to the upper chambers from the interior"

which shows what a sad state it was in, and gloom descended when Messrs. Wheeler, the Reading building firm, put in their tender for £1,800; and even when modifications reduced this to £1,400 it was felt to be too much. The interval while Gilbert Scott was modifying his plans inevitably saw counter-suggestions. Mr. Clark following a report from the Improvement Committee, observed that

"it appeared to him to be perfectly useless laying out this money on the old building. There was a main street wanting repair"

especially as it would only "perpetuate a nuisance and keep up a building that was neither beautiful nor useful". These sentiments were disregarded, as had been the suggestion that the building be demolished and its stone arch re-erected in the renovated Forbury.

Time was however, slipping by, and while adverse comment was made on the parsimony of Reading folk, and Mr. Scott seemed dilatory over producing his revised plans. the gateway was rapidly degenerating. By

December 1860 it had to be shored up and the public advised not to pass under this now tottering fabric"; water was percolating and a further fall on the north side was imminent. In January 1861 a letter in the Times made a general appeal for subscriptions, as

"all travellers by the Great Western must be familiar with this reminiscence of the olden time"

But by March there had been little success, evoking the justified response that

"This does not speak much for the professed lovers of ancient architecture throughout the country who were so ready to come forward and charge the town of Reading with an act of gross vandalism, when there was a rumour that the gateway was about to be destroyed".

Meanwhile, the road had been entirely closed to carriages and pedestrians, one of the southern buttresses had fallen and also "the pillar base of the arch itself". In February 1861, following a storm and further collapse

"a number of men have been engaged in taking down the dangerous and more modern portions of it".

March, however, was to be the crucial month. Wheeler's estimate, based

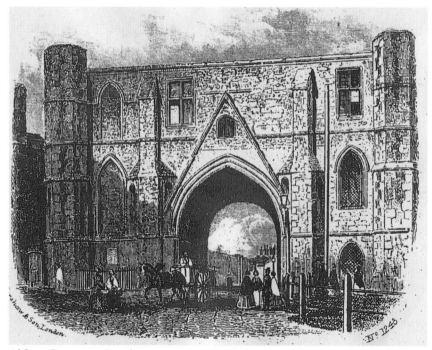

Abbey Gateway, Reading
North face c 1850.

The Inner Gateway, Reading Abbey, restored 1859.
North face after 1861.

on new specifications and so reduced to £1,000, was accepted by the Improvement Committee and work was at last authorised. There was some dismay at its slow start, but it thereafter proceeded apace: old material taken down was stacked in the Forbury and rebuilding proper started in May. By August, when the Mayor opened the Forbury he could refer to "the handsome gateway before us" and that he had voted for its demolition. joking that

"while the jury were sitting upon it for life or "death it attempted suicide".

But he now believed that

"it could be the best and the first of the few architectural ornaments they had in the town".

Within six months from the start of the rebuilding the exterior work was virtually finished, to what would seem general satisfaction

"The Reading Abbey Gateway is now seen in all its fine proportions, as accumulated soil has been removed and the road levelled. . . Certainly this building is one of the most beautiful specimens of the Norman architectural period which we shall find in the south-west of England. The Messrs. Wheeler have most admirably realized the drawings of Mr. Gilbert Scott, and when the interior fittings are finished we shall have a very noble building".

So, thanks to Scott and Wheeler, Reading now had an admirable piece of medieval architecture. The main work was completed in January 1862 with the putting in of windows, frames and glass; by May only some internal fittings remained to be done, and plans were already well advanced for the letting of the large room there.

By 1862 all standing remains of the abbey, except the surviving parts of the mill, were in the hands of the Corporation, for the dormitory of the old guesthouse, used by Reading School, was in effect under their control. The first sixty years of the nineteenth century were years of fundamental change in almost all aspects of life, and by 1860 local government had responsibilities that would have been largely incomprehensible in 1800: public expectation of local authority activity was quite different and had been steadily rising. Reading's authorities were, in this new attention to public amenities, as they had been in the past, neither the best nor the worst in the land. In the outcome they had done well, if hesitantly, as far as they had gone, but it was a lost opportunity that the other part of the abbey site was disposed of elsewhere.

VI

The Town acquires the Forbury: late 18th century–1861

By the late eighteenth century the Forbury was, as we have seen, the only portion of the former abbey actively used, if not owned, by the town. It was the focal point for communal activities that increased, and took on a martial tinge from 1793 when the start of the long war with France saw a surge in military and naval affairs. The militia, a part-time national organization, now usually trained on Bulmershe Heath, but the Reading Volunteers, local men for local defence, exercised in the Forbury. In 1794 the mayor, Martin Annesley, its captain, gave a banquet in the Town Hall for three hundred guests including its officers, who attended "in their full uniforms". The nearest they came to active service was in 1795 when they were called from their exercising in the Forbury to put down a riot between townspeople and Irish Dragoons, who were quartered in Reading. The Volunteers were a source of local pride and in 1797, to celebrate Admiral Duncan's victory over the Dutch

> "the Reading Volunteers were drawn out of the Forbury whence they marched to the Town Hall and fired three excellent volleys".

Their standard was clearly high, for volley-firing with flint-lock muskets, even the famous Brown Bess, was not easy. The Volunteers received pay from the government, but the men's uniforms were provided by public subscription. However, in 1798, with the threat of invasion felt to be even more present, an unpaid voluntary force, the Loyal Reading Volunteers or the Armed Association, was formed "from among the principal inhabitants who were no longer averse from taking the ranks". They usually numbered some 150 and provided colourful entertainment in the Forbury, for

> "their uniforms were blue with scarlet facings, caps and helmets; they were provided with an excellent band of music, and a pair of elegant colours presented to the corps by a lady".

Their activities added to the predominating military affairs in the Forbury. In February 1789 the supplementary militia paraded and the ballot for the half selected to serve was held at Mr. Andrew's house there. In May the Reading Armed Association "consisting of upwards of 200 of the most respectable tradesmen and housekeepers of this borough" paraded there in uniform, then marched into the Market Place with the mayor at their head. They paraded again in June and in the same month the Reading Volunteers "went through various manoeuvres and firings there". In October both bodies paraded to celebrate Nelson's victory, and a week later they were joined for the same purpose by the Woodley Cavalry and the 15th Light Dragoons – a colourful spectacle – and "three excellent volleys were then fired in rotation". "Three excellent volleys" were again fired there by the Volunteers and the Association in June 1799 to mark the king's birthday, after which the Association "had a field day in the Forbury". Both bodies continued to exercise there: In May 1800, for example

> "In the afternoon the Reading Volunteers assembled in the Forbury and after going through various evolutions proceeded to the Market Place . . . on Tuesday afternoon the Reading Armed Association were drawn out in the Forbury where they went through their manoeuvres in a manner highly honorable to themselves".

Royal birthdays were popular events and chances for displays by the local military: in 1801, for example, the Volunteers paraded in the Forbury and fired three volleys; their band played 'God Save The King' at intervals and the many spectators "expressed the utmost satisfaction". In October of that year celebrations for the preliminaries of peace produced one of the Forbury's more colourful episodes:

> "As soon as church was concluded the Forbury became the scene of most animating triumph and was crowded with persons of all descriptions to witness the military honours and exploits of both the horse and foot soldiery. A detachment of the 7th Dragoons quartered here, the Woodley Cavalry, the Reading Volunteers and the Association were drawn up in grand and judicious arrangement. Uniform and repeated volleys in alternate succession – discharge of cannon – the heroic music of bands – and the loud acclamations of an immense multitude vibrated the air with patriotic joy and gladness".

But the disembodying of the militia, Volunteers and the Association in spring 1802 proved premature, and the renewal of the war saw them all back on parade. Training does not seem to have suffered, for in December 1803 the two last

> "were mustered and inspected in the Forbury. Sir Nathaniel Dukinfield was highly satisfied at the appearance of both corps and the manner in which they performed their evolutions".

In 1804 both bodies paraded in the Forbury, although on separate days, to receive their colours, the Loyal Volunteers receiving theirs from the mayor, the Marchioness of Blandford presenting theirs to the Volunteers. In August of that year there was an unusual meeting, when the Oxford Loyal Volunteers met the Reading Volunteers in the Forbury, and the combined body marched to Bulmershe Heath. Reading's Armed Association had gone by the end of 1805, and in 1806 the sovereign's birthday was marked by a colourful and professional celebration when

> "the Royal Horse Guards Blues paraded in the Forbury at 12 o'clock, completely equipped and mounted, and fired three *feux-de-joie-* in honour of the day".

The Volunteers, however, continued in existence. In June 1806 they paraded "to fire powder", when leave of absence was only granted to those "particularly engaged in the hay harvest". At various times in the same and the next year they paraded "with flints for firing", and at other times "with fixed flints for muster and inspection". The plea that "every man is expected to attend" suggests that zeal was lacking for what was by now a pointless activity, all danger of invasion having disappeared. In June 1809 they took part in a grand parade

> "In this town the king's birthday was celebrated with the most lively marks of loyalty and patriotism. The Woodley Cavalry under Captain Goldring, the Royal Berkshire Regiment under the Marquis of Blandford and the Volunteers under Colonel Newbery paraded in the Forbury which was gaily "decked with trophies of naval victory, won by our gallant townsman, Captain Bolton, a display peculiarly gratifying"

But it turned out to be their last ceremonial parade. Later that month there was a mutiny among the local militia during exercises in the Forbury, for they had been refused their "marching guinea". Some of the Volunteers parading there urged them on: the militia's commander complained to the War Office and in July, as a result, the Volunteers were dismissed "without the smallest remuneration or compliment". So in October it was left to the Royal Horse Guards to fire three volleys to mark the fiftieth anniversary of the king's accession. On that occasion, tables were erected in the Forbury, where a "fine, fat ox" was roasted, there were three barrels of strong beer and free bread. Thereafter the military element hardly figured in the celebrations. In November 1813, to mark Napoleon's defeat at the battle of Leigzig, the crowd, after a grand firework display and the burning of Napoleon's effigy.

> "then moved in procession to the house of our chief magistrate in the Forbury and gave three hearty cheers".

On that occasion, the firework display far exceeded anything of the kind previously seen in the town, and the wetness of the day put no blight on the amusements. At the peace celebrations of 1814; 6,000 were fed at tables in the streets, and

> "The evening will be devoted to the exhibition of rural and ludicrous sports which will take place in the Forbury at 6 o'clock consisting of donkey races, jumping and running in sacks. a pig hunt, gingling grinning and smoking matches, dancing etc",

and it was later reported that "they went off with *éclat*".

The most regular events now established in the Forbury were three of the four annual fairs, held in February, May and September: the fourth, the July cattle fair, was at this time held mainly in other parts of the town. The February and May fairs were mainly for cattle and horses, February's being the more important, and they both included some popular entertainment. But the most important of all was the Michaelmas fair of September. This covered everything – cattle and horses, hops, miscellaneous goods, hiring of servants, cheese and entertainment. The importance of the last two features led to its being known as the Reading Cheese Fair, with its accompanying Pleasure Fair. In former days a thousand or more tons of cheese displayed for sale had been usual, but during the earlier nineteenth century the average was some 500 tons. At times much would remain unsold, as in 1802 or 1848; in 1837 'several wagon-loads went back to the dairy country"; in 1841 it was noted that "the cheese went off heavily during the day", indicating very sluggish sales; in 1846 "about two tons of unclaimed cheese" were being held by the police; in 1847 dealers refused to reduce their prices, so although the cheese "was certainly of a finer and riper quality than ordinary" much was taken back. Bad weather at times impeded trade; in 1814, for example, the poor supply was partly due to "the badness of navigation", likewise in 1829 when "a very high flood" on the Thames stopped the boats bringing cheese. In 1835 "heavy and incessant rain" stopped nearly all transactions; and it was worse in 1852, for the morning's rain "had somewhat injured" the cheese itself. The cheese was pitched on the Grammar School's play area, the rest of the Forbury being available for the pleasure fair and for livestock. Animals for sale included "droves of Shetland or forest ponies" and pigs, besides the usual horses and cattle. Horses, especially, were usually there in quantity if not quality, although no other year was as bad as 1829 when there was "the most miserable show of horses ever seen" with many "wretched hacks".

The Michaelmas Pleasure Fair was a major annual event with stalls in the Market Place and stalls and entertainment in the Forbury. Before 1798 entertainments had cluttered the streets, but in that year the many "caravans of wild beasts and shows of other descriptions" were ordered into the Forbury, a much more convenient practice and one followed in subsequent years. The pleasure fair had been subdued during the war years, but with peace it revived and expanded. The year 1814, when "of stalls and shows there was never remembered so many", saw the first visit by Gillman and Atkin's Grand Menagerie "consisting of the most Wonderful Productions of Nature", admission 1s. ladies and gentlemen, 6d. children and servants. Among other attractions was a Camera Obscura "on the largest scale":

> "As a commanding situation is desirable it will be stationed on the green in the Forbury where the public will not be inconvenienced by the cattle".

The often unfavourable weather did not damp the pleasure fairs, which steadily expanded. In 1821

> "exhibits of wild beasts, giants, dwarfs, etc exceeded those at any former fair"

although the rain reduced takings. The 1823 show included

> "Adam's celebrated equestrian troop, Wombwell's extensive menagerie and the Vauxhall gardens in miniature"

the last occupying a space 180 by 50 feet. Wombwell's was a never-failing favourite and always received high praise, no matter what the criticism of other shows. After Mr. Wombwell died – and was appropriately buried with a lion on his sarcophagus – Mr. Edmonds took over "the best of the three collections of the late Mr. Wombwell", but by 1856 it was "Mrs. Wombwell's Menagerie"; and it still maintained its popularity in 1859 when it was noted that "Mrs. Wombwell has travelled upwards of fifty years in this line". Not only was Wombwell's Menagerie the leading entertainment, but their brass band always received the highest praise. In 1841, for example,

> "The playing of Mr. Wombwell's delightful brass band afforded as usual a rich treat to hundreds of attentive and approving hearers"

Exceptional entertainment was provided in 1846 when "the lion queen who accompanied Mr. Wombwell's Menagerie was, of course, the centre of attraction"; and again in the next year

> "the town was enlivened by the entrance of Mr. Wombwell's Menagerie, headed by the brass band and conducted by the youthful Miss Chapman on an elephant".

Each year produced some unique feature in the pleasure fair. In 1814 it was a "tremendous serpent" – a live, sixteen foot boa-constrictor. In 1826, among the promised entertainments

"Mr. SCOWTON'S ROYAL PAVILION will be numbered. . . His scenery and performances of such a superior description as to command the most unqualified approbation".

In the event, the verdict was that "Mr. Scowton's theatre should not be tolerated beyond this evening". In 1829 there was an unusual entertainment when

"In the pleasure fair we had a great novelty; the Dissenters of all denominations turned out their pastors, and in various stations the learned gentlemen were holding forth to numerous auditories".

although

"notwithstanding this work of supererogation Wombwell's lions and black tigers, Samwell's horsemanship, Chapel's Gymnastics, Wax Work Exhibition, tumblers etc, etc., had a great share of public favour".

In 1837 "an ingenious application of mechanism to wax figures attracted great attention", a description elaborated for the May Fair of 1844:

"Among the chief attractions of the Forbury may be ranked Mr. Purchase's Collection of Wax Figures, not only on account of the novelty of the subjects produced (which include the murder of Sir William McNaughton during the insurrection at Cabool, and the death of Nelson), but from the circumstances of its being worked by powerful machinery to represent nature, so that all classes of visitors will, no doubt, be both amused and instructed".

In 1843 "the female dwarf (19 inches only in height)" was the great attraction. In 1852, in addition to Wombwell's

"the other large shows were a circus and a theatre, in the latter of which on Wednesday evening the tragedy of Macbeth was done in about 10 minutes, to the great delight of crowded audiences. Wizards, fortune-telling ponies, peep shows, etc. etc. completely filled the ground allotted to this part of the fair".

In 1840 a recruiting party of the Rifles, aided by "an excellent brass band" persuaded nearly 50 young men to enlist during the two days of the fair. By 1858 a reduction in available space and the largest pleasure fair for many years caused such crowding that "Mr. Cooke's equestrian establishment had to be erected in an adjoining meadow" but by then the end was in sight for the Forbury Pleasure Fairs.

Crime at the fairs was kept to a minimum by the vigilance of the magistrates. In earlier times, order was kept by any available military; at the Candlemas Fair of 1794 the 15th Light Dragoons did guard duty, their numbers including the young S.T. Coleridge, the later famous poet, who was serving as a volunteer. In 1821 an "active officer from Bow Street" came for the May fair However, the development of a local police force was the best discouragement to crime, as in 1841 when

> "a gang of the swell mob arrived during the fair, but their movements were closely regarded by our excellent police force"

and as in 1843 when a great number of "prigs" were thwarted by the police, who were "exceedingly active and vigilant". Pickpockets once described as "light-fingered gentry called divers", were the main nuisance. Those caught received summary punishment; four apprehended in 1830 were sentenced to a month on the treadmill, and two in 1834 got three months' hard labour. What must have been typical of fair time happened to a north Wiltshire dairyman in 1830 who, retiring with "a nymph of the pave", was eased of the £65 he had taken for his cheese. In the same year a lad foolishly let a "sharper" try out a mare; he galloped away down the Bath Road and disappeared, and wise advice was given in 1814:

> "valuable horses should be taken out of the neighbouring meadows as gangs of horse-stealers are always lurking about several days before and after fairs".

However, new transport heralded basic changes. Reading's Great Western Railway station was opened in March 1840, and for the September fair of that year

> "the arrivals by the various trains were quite extraordinary, particularly those from the metropolis, the carriages of which were absolutely thronged"

and in 1858 visitors still flocked from afar:

> "Each of the railway companies ran a special train from London and intermediate stations on Tuesday last. The Southern conveyed hither 827 persons, the South-Eastern about 400, and the Great Western also brought a large number".

However, railways had an adverse effect on the cheese fair. In 1840, as well as the first passengers, the first cheese came by train and in 1849 it was complained that

"Large quantities of the best cheese were disposed of at the station to London dealers, without being brought to the fair".

More seriously, increasing ease of communication killed the ponderous annual fairs, first in favour of monthly and bi-monthly markets, then of the cheese factor "from whom the grocer receives a constant and regular supply", so that by 1859 the cheese at Reading's fair was reduced to some 57½ tons. The end came in 1860, and in 1861 a small quantity of cheese was exhibited in the Market Place. Thereafter a cheese market was to be held in the Corn Exchange. And the sale of cattle, from 1861 removed to the new Cattle Market, was felt to be a great improvement.

Besides the pleasure fairs there were many other public entertainments in the Forbury. From 1814 The Drum and Fife Band of the Royal Berks Militia played there and the staff drilled. At times the full militia paraded: it

"was ordered to be drawn out and assembled in the Forbury . . . there to be trained and exercised for a period of 28 days"

although in November 1852

"so violent have been the rains that they could not be assembled for the preparatory drill"

and in the next November, fog then rain, caused the men to be sent home. In 1854 they were a weedy lot. Two hundred had enlisted into the line – the Crimean War against Russia had begun in March – and concerning those left and now on parade

"We cannot speak very favourably of the appearance or behaviour of a considerable portion of these levies whose first business appeared to be indulging in intoxication and using language of the most disgusting character".

They markedly improved however, and a large number of spectators assembled in the Forbury to view their final parade. There was no music at the militia's drill in 1855 but by 19 May "clothing for the band" had been received from London, and they played "some lively airs" on Forbury Hill A month later this, their depot band, led the Royal Berks Militia, which had just returned from Corfu at the end of the Crimean War, from the station to the Forbury but, unfortunately, "during one of the heaviest showers we have had for a long time". The last assembly by the militia in the Forbury was in 1860, although stores remained and the band continued to play there. Even so, military entertainment in the Forbury was not lost, for in the same year a new body, the Volunteer Rifle Corps, "marched to the Forbury headed by a brass band and subsequently returned to the Corn

Exchange". By 1861 plans were in hand by the Volunteers to form a brass band to play twice a week in the Forbury, and it was there and playing on Forbury Hill by the next year.

Circuses visited at other than fair times, and they and firework displays were standard entertainment. For circuses and similar displays a large tent, called an amphitheatre or pavilion, was erected in the Forbury. These pavilions could be elaborate affairs. Van Amburgh's show of June 1841 involving animals and carriages, was performed in one

> "containing 10,130 square feet of canvas, fitted up with seats covered with ornamental drapery and calculated to hold from two thousand to three thousand persons".

Admission was 1s. each with seats 6d. extra. "Wondrous feats of horsemanship in an enormous and elegant amphitheatre" were offered in 1842 by Brice and North's British and American Equestrian Company. In May 1847 Hughes's Royal Mammoth and Grand Oriental Establishment was led into the town by

> "the Egyptian Dragon Chariot or perambulating Temple of Isis and Osiris, purchased at the enormous cost of 200,000 piastres, drawn by four gigantic camels".

Crowds of townsfolk gathered to watch and to see the performance advertised "for one day only". Unkind comment suggested that this was too long, for the only thing worth watching was the procession, the equestrian events were pathetic, the only person to laugh at the clown was himself, and far too many spectators were crammed into the tent. But failure was rare and among successful entertainers were big names from the circus world: Batty's, Hengler's, especially with its "pony races with monkeys for jockeys", Hernandez and Co's, Cook's, Cushing's, Bells and, near the end, Sanger's Zoological Hippodrome and Mammoth Circus, which made a dramatic entry

> "headed by the brass band of the establishment in full costume seated in their magnificent musical chariot".

The last circus performance in the Forbury was in November 1860, Howes and Cushing's circus finishing on a satisfactory note when

> "the drolleries of the educated mules Pete and Barney created hearty laughter".

There were a number of firework displays, the most successful being those of Mr. Gingell of, then late of, Royal Vauxhall Gardens. He staged a very successful show"by private and public subscription" in November

1831, the high point being "the ascension of a magnificent Montgolfier balloon which rose from the Green to an immense altitude". He surpassed himself in June 1833, although it was felt to have been a bit drawn out, with music and illuminations on the Forbury Green, which was "thronged with fashion and elegance" while to dash the hopes of those who hoped to avoid paying "canisters to receive the public subscriptions of persons on the outside of the Green" were circulated. The high spot was "the paralyzing ascension and descension of Madame de Irvine on the fiery rope" and comment was ecstatic:

> "The effect of the appearance of this lady at an altitude of forty feet among the foliage of the trees illuminated with the Bengal lights was more beautiful than can be described".

In 1836 an ambitious sixty-foot ascension came to nothing when the mainstays of the fiery rope gave way, although the Montgolfier balloon and the military band were very successful; sadly, the replacement show planned for the following weekend did not take place as no-one had asked the mayor's permission to stage it. The following year Gingell gave a show in the Forbury for the benefit of the Royal Berkshire Hospital, although the keen north-east wind reduced the audience; conversely his show in October 1847 was enthusiastically attended despite a day of cold and rain. On that occasion there were edifying activities:

> "After the fireworks an exhibition of dissolving views, the oxy-hydrogen gas microscope and the chromotrope or Chinese kaleidoscope took place in the Town Hall, which was both fashionably and numerously attended".

However, not all firework shows were successful. Signor Duvalli's in 1843 was marked by an unruly crowd and few fireworks; and at the peace celebrations in May 1856, marking the end of the Crimean War,

> "Of the fireworks little can be said as they were, except for the rockets, few and far between",

a poor reward for standing for two hours on a bleak May evening.

A number of exhibitions took place. One closely associated with recent events occurred in August 1816 in a building erected in the Forbury, and consisted of

> "the military carriage and all its curious apparatus in which Bonaparte made his campaign in Russia and in which he escaped at Waterloo"

and it was accompanied by his coachman, who had lost an arm there, and by the postillion who had gone with Napoleon to Elba. In 1840 there was an exhibition "consisting of models of several celebrated ruins" which "reflects infinite credit on the taste and industry of the proprietor". In 1841 the skeleton of "the Royal British Whale" was exhibited with various other animal skeletons and "the singular preservod bodies of the Peruvian chiefs and oil paintings". At 1s. for gentry and 6d. for tradespeople and servants it was "very fairly patronized". In 1860 Mr. Rarey gave a successful lecture and practical demonstration of horse training in a "spacious marquee" there. Possibly the Forbury's most dramatic event of these years took place on 3 August 1823 with the balloon ascent of Mr. Green, "the celebrated English aeronaut", who survived over 500 ascents before his retirement in the 1850s. Before a packed audience drawn from miles around

> "the band struck up 'God save the King' and at seven minutes to 5 o'clock the balloon rose majestically amid the acclamations of innumerable spectators. who appeared struck with astonishment at the novelty, beauty and magnificence of the spectacle . . . "Mr. Green was standing up in the car bowing to the spectators, and Mr. Simmonds waved the flag in token of the confidence he felt in his new and perilous situation".

Mr. Henry Simonds of Broad Street had bravely volunteered. The balloon landed at North Mimms, Herts. Occasionally activity was of a more serious nature, as in 1809 when there were varying views over celebrating the 50th anniversary of George III's accession. A group of leading townsmen planned to meet on Forbury Hill

> "independently of the mayor who has refused to call a public meeting to take into account the propriety of celebrating the 25th instant, being the 50th anniversary of His Majesty's accession – and also to assert and maintain inviolate the Right of the People to assemble and express their own sentiments in their own style, on all public occasions"

and the meeting was well attended. Although their objections were not met, the subsequent day of celebration "was spent with utmost harmony". There was a non-controversial but edifying occasion on Whit Monday 1843 when

> "members of the various Benefit Clubs in this town assembled in the Forbury"

They subsequently paraded round the town with music and flags, but as was so often the case in Reading celebrations "the day was extremely unfavourable for the display". On the morning of the Michaelmas Fair of 1820, a strange object, identified as an extraordinary meteor, was seen:

"It appeared first to be a pointed star, rather larger than a crown piece, and continued so for one and a half hours, seeming stationary over Forbury Hill".

and in 1841, after a severe hailstorm, "a singular shower of fish . . . called tittlebats or pricklebacks" were found alive there. However, in 1815, a donkey race in the Forbury was found an unsatisfying substitute for the Reading Races.

Royal and outstanding occasions were celebrated there. To mark the 50th year of George III's reign

"a very fine fat ox and three barrels of beer, the gift of the master butchers, together with a proportionate quantity of bread, the gift of the master bakers, was spread upon the tables erected in the Forbury".

Free food marked the peace celebrations of July 1814 when "the sports in the Forbury went off with eclat". Rural sports and fireworks in the Forbury delighted a large crowd at the coronation celebrations of 1831, although the day "partook of the usual varied character of this uncertain clime". "Innocent sports" likewise figured in celebrations marking the 1832 Reform Bill. Celebrations in 1838 for Victoria's Coronation lasted "from dawn to a very late hour", the Forbury being the scene of a lively and impressive show:

"In the afternoon the rural amusements were resumed in the Forbury, and much diversion occasioned by the dipping in flour, wheeling blindfolded, climbing for mutton, pig-chasing, etc. etc.".

In the evening there took place on the Green

"one of the most brilliant illuminations ever perhaps exhibited out of the metropolis . . . upwards of 8,000 lamps were employed"

and

"the promenade was densely crowded with a most respectable assembly and enlivened by some very lively airs from a powerful band".

The day finished with a firework display on Forbury Hill. Most were pleased but a disgruntled element had wanted a regatta. The last of these old-style festivities, to mark the peace of 1856, had, by contrast a few rustic exhibitions" and a poor firework display.

There were a number of dwellers in the Forbury. ranging from the wealthy to the averagely well off. In 1813 the mayor lived there, and in 1829 the Paving Commissioners reduced the rateable value of Thomas

Grint Curteis's house there: possibly it was just a coincidence that he was then mayor. The situation in the Forbury was certainly desirable: in 1825, a house for sale was advertised as

> "standing in the Forbury Green, a situation close to the town, but perfectly rural, and commanding an uninterrupted view of picturesque scenery".

In 1837 a substantial house there sandwiched between the church and the Literary Institute and reading room was let, and

> "it has a fine prospect over the Oxfordshire hills and the Forbury: the situation is considered by medical men to be remarkably healthy"

A number of genteel trades were plied there especially education. in 1801 Mr Bath, an assistant at Reading Grammar School there, took "an airy and commodious" house for taking boarders: by 1839 he was running his own preparatory school – Abbey House School – in the Forbury. Mr. Street. who had his own school in the Forbury, likewise accommodated Grammar School boarders. In 1841 the Misses Street had a short-lived school there, likewise Miss Edge. Longer-lived was that run by Miss Curteis and Miss Grint at the Abbey House for Young Ladies. As late as 1838 Mrs. Bradley's Preparatory School for Young Gentlemen – she could take 12, all treated with "tender attention" and prepared for Eton, Harrow and King's College, London – moved to Forbury House. Among others active was Mr. Lawrance who, by 1830, made and sold rheumatic powders at No. 4: they were also sold by Mrs. Meadows of the Forbury, who had effected a marvellous cure for Martha Rowbottom's rheumatic gout. Ladies desiring to purchase Mrs. Lloyd Gibbon's Anatomical Stays, that

> "from their nicety of adjustment and peculiar construction are adapted to every age and variety of form"

were advised to make early application to No. 3 the Forbury. But these commercial activities died away, and the practising of his profession by Mr. Jordan, "resident surgical and mechanical dentist" in 1855 at No. 7. was unusual as, indeed, was the taking in 1853 of a house near the Grammar School for storing militia equipment. Among reasons for their dying away was the reduction in the number of dwellings in the Forbury itself and along the Green there in the 1840s and 50s with the construction of the new Assize Court and the expansion of Sutton's, Reading's famous seed firm. The public had previously been welcome to view their excellent tulips, etc but there was, by 1844, a new and pleasing amenity as Sutton's gardens had been extended from the Market Place to Forbury Green, making "a most agreeable promenade for lovers of horticultural Beauty". But activity by the Reading Auction Mart on Forbury Green, selling "live

West Side of the Forbury, c 1805

and dead stock" – in 1841 the latter included 6 gigs, phaeton, bath chair and carts – "detracted from the amenities".

A main function of the Forbury was to provide an area for the young to play, even if this took the form of throwing stones, and the more mature to perambulate. Popular feeling was alert for any encroachment. In 1813 claims were again advanced by the headmaster of the Grammar School, on this occasion the redoubtable Dr. Valpy, for the exclusive use by the school of part of the Forbury as a playground, which evoked the spirited response

> "that the inhabitants of this borough have an established right to walk, exercise and divert themselves in and upon the Forbury, and every part of it, at their free will and pleasure . . ."

and the claims were finally abandoned after a series of fights between his pupils and local youth. In 1818 an auctioneer selling horses in the Forbury near the school was successfully warned off by the headmaster. But Mr. Winkworth, "an intrepid assertor of the sights and privileges of the borough" immediately took his horse and cart there and several times drove past the master's door to emphasise this as a right. Even more exclusive claims were put forward in 1851 when headmaster Appleton was accused of assault when he demanded the removal of a gig being repaired on what he considered to be 'his' part of the Forbury. In his annoyance he told his pupils to pitch their cricket stumps in the Forbury whenever they desired, claiming that he paid rent to Colonel Blagrave for the whole Blagrave part. In his desire to score a point, he over⎯ked the sensitivity of the townsfolk towards anything they regarded as an encroachment on their rights in the Forbury. So, a week later, nearly a thousand inhabitants, young and old, held sports and games, including "a spirited game of cricket"

> "upon that portion of the Forbury used as a playground of the pupils educating at Reading Grammar School"

A subscription was raised then and there, mainly for buying beer, by eight in the evening the assembly had grown very large, and there was, wisely, "no interference by any party" and nothing more was heard of the claim. However, more formal cricket matches did take place in the Forbury, as for many years it was the home of Reading Cricket Club. Other encroachments such as that by Lord Bexley's agents of the path behind Forbury Hill in 1833; or that by the South-Eastern Railway in 1852, when about five feet of the greensward beyond the old wall were occupied, including the "public promenade" there, were quickly checked.

However, it was to be some time before serious attention extended to its condition. Opinion in 1809 considered it

> ". . . one of the pleasantest spots in the county. It is called the Forbury: on the south and west sides it is enclosed with houses, a part of the churchyard, and the magnificent remains of the Abbey which have hitherto bade defiance to devouring time and the still more destructive energies of man. On the north side is a long terrace walk, bounded by a low wall, affording a delightful view of the Oxfordshire hills . . . Charming as this spot is, its beauties are all lost to the inhabitants: you will scarcely credit the assertion when I tell you this delightful terrace is for a great way bordered by an enormous dunghill, formed by the scavenger and the nightman. The road leading through it is mended, or rather deteriorated with broken bricks, tiles etc., etc., collected from the ruins of old buildings, laid up in this place by different workmen, who seem to consider it rather as a deposit for their rubbish than a promenade for ladies. In front of the houses is a plot of grass of a semi-circular form, in part surrounded by palisadoes, and in part by a muddy ditch, the general receptacle of dead dogs, cats and carrion of all kinds, sufficient to build a pestilence in this otherwise salubrious spot. Attempts have at times been made to improve this pleasant place but without effect which must be the case, till the Corporation remove the fairs, annually held here, to a more convenient situation . . ."

but it was to be some two generations before his hopes were realised. Other "great nuisances" noted there were broken glass bottles and "the filth arising from cattle being turned out to graze". A sonnet in 1827 'The Forbury on a Misty Evening in Autumn', by Thomas Noon Talfourd, disregarded the less salubrious features:

> "Soft uplands that in youth's admiring days

Look'd mountain-like and distant, fain once more
Would I behold you, but the Autumn hoar
Hath veiled your pensive groves in evening haze".

Complaints were still running strongly in 1843 when notice was drawn to "the dangerous and filthy condition of the ditch" surrounding Forbury Green, and that "a heap of rubbish of the most nauseous kind has been suffered to accumulate near the footway". Nor was the track there any better, for a horse, slipping into a hole, precipitated itself, gig and gentleman into the ditch. It was not until 1847 that a substantial fence was erected, but only after a horse and chaise had backed into the ditch, and a spectator fallen in during a fireworks display; it was, though, a sign of changing attitudes that it was felt that with the passing of the anticipated "Sanitary Bill" this fencing activity would be insufficient. At the other end of the site the dilapidated and dangerous wall was a matter of complaint; and rough behaviour spread from the Forbury, necessitating the erection of a boundary rail round St. Lawrence's churchyard to keep out those who "rudely trampled over the ground disfiguring its tombs etc."

However, anticipation that legislation would produce significant change was correct. The Public Health Act of 1848 allowed the setting up of local Boards of Health, and by 1852 major change was pending in Reading's relationship with the Forbury. The mayor, at a committee meeting, observed that the whole Forbury was in a disgraceful state, that liability for repairs should be ascertained and, significantly, that the Board (of Health) had the power to purchase land. His observation was in part caused by the way the pedestrian road to the station of the Reigate Railway, just to the north of the Forbury, was being cut up by vehicles heading there. In February 1852, at a wet cattle fair, parts of the Forbury were virtually impassable from the depth of the mud, but over a year later, in October 1853, the Board of Health again reported on

> "the disgraceful state of the Forbury caused by vehicles being driven across it to and from the railway station"

and it was decided to seek the co-operation of the owner, Colonel Blagrave, to such theoretical good effect that by December plans were in hand for a good carriage road "within the circumference of the Green", where the ditch was to be abolished, railway traffic was to be kept within bounds and there was to be space for public recreation.

But what really turned the Corporation's thoughts towards purchase was the Forbury Hill. By 1799 this feature was a local, if somewhat exposed, amenity

> "That beautiful spot, Forbury Hill, having been lately embellished with railings, etc at a considerable expense and which was cheerfully

Forbury Hills and Abbey Gate, c. 1800

defrayed by the voluntary contributions of the inhabitants of this town, we were lamenting to see the depredations made upon it, the last few evenings by persons who have been observed to be loitering about . . ."

This first erection of railings there had been done in 1790, partly by the work of prisoners from the county gaol. In 1805 it was reported that the Hill "by the attention of the present mayor is rendered a commodious and pleasant resort for the inhabitants of the town" but by 1813 a poet described it as "this neglected hill" and continued

"And thou, poor Mount, how shalt thou fare the while?
Will no protecting safeguard bid thee smile?
No friendly hand arise to fence thee round?
To heal thy deep distresses none be found?".

Relief works in the hard winter of 1816–17 resulted, before the money ran out, in a retaining wall around its base, and soon a friendly hand did arise, for over the next few years the then tenant, Mr. Joshua Vines, worked and paid, voluntarily, to keep it in much-needed repair, for it had "so long been suffered to crumble away under the mischievous pranks of idle boys". In 1830 it was suggested that townsfolk should subscribe to the cost of an iron railing

> "without which support his work will soon be trodden down by cattle and mischievous children".

He did get heavily criticized in 1833 for planting two oak saplings on top as out of keeping with its elm trees, potentially damaging its views and impeding children's enjoyment of "the soft verdant sward with which the hill is so richly clothed". The "much decayed" elm trees, however, could be a liability, as in 1836 when a large branch nearly injured a gentleman and broke the iron fence, repaired by the long-suffering Mr. Vines; and again, as some twenty years later, when one of the "venerable elms" shed a large branch almost on to a gentleman and some children. There was also one rather useless street light on it. A commentator in 1831 waxed lyrical over the views from it, across and up and down the Thames Valley where "the neat little village of Caversham is seen to particular advantage", but the tone was rather different in February 1838 when

> "Great activity prevails on the site of the Western Railway near this town. The embankment . . . has deprived the Forbury Promenade of its chief attraction, the view of the windy Thames. Forbury Hill, however, yet overlooks the unsightly obstruction".

although by 1840 it was thought that the Forbury with its view of the trains would become "a very fashionable promenade".

The rails of the hill were temporarily removed in 1845 for more soil "to be pitched in the hollow" to make a level surface for the planting of ornamental trees, and it was hoped that inhabitants of Reading would contribute a few loads of mould, but all was not well in May 1852 when, at a Council meeting Mr. Dunn remarked that

> "the time of year is coming on when the inhabitants of the town would like to enjoy the fresh breeze up there . . ."

and who was responsible for repairing or replacing the seats? The town clerk pointed out that despite the iron rails being put there by public subscription, it was private property, but there was worse the next year when

> "In the night of Wednesday, a portion of the north side of the Hill bulged, and forced out a considerable quantity of the brickwork leaving the walk in an unsafe state: this slip possibly occurred from the previous heavy rains. The custom of carpet-beating on the railings should be prevented as it shakes the foundation which supports it".

Repairs must have been done by the owner or tenant, but by July 1854 the situation was becoming difficult. The tenant had erected a beer-shop on top of it, and had erected "pot-house signposts"; he had taken a pick-axe to the public seats, and had ordered those not wanting ale or cigars to leave. The town clerk got himself into a legal tangle over the matter, and it was even hinted, although in general terms, that he put "obliging any party who may possess peculiar influence" before "the rights of a native town". It was hardly surprising that an element in the town took the law into its own hands. At the end of August the sign-post was sawn down and a riotous and noisy gathering of some seven to eight hundred people "refreshed by supplies of beer" demolished the landlord's table, smashed his window and demolished the gas-light. The crowd dispersed at about ten o'clock, but it was feared that this was but the first demonstration of many. It was these events that, almost certainly, finally galvanized the Board of Health into taking the decisive step. Earlier in the year the owner, Mr. Wheble, had expressed the intention of selling the Hill and the nearby part of the Forbury, and in April influential local opinion clearly expressed itself in favour of purchase. In July it was remarked that the Forbury was "generally uninviting", especially as it was still "driven over in all directions by the traffic of the South-Eastern station" – Colonel Blagrave's efforts had clearly not been effective – and that at least the plot of ground now available could be made into a promenade "judiciously restricted to the well-behaved classes". The Hill could form "a retreat for the lounger and a relaxation for the busy" while the central part could be railed off for games for the young, and specified roads kept for access to the station. All this would benefit the inhabitants, and

> "prove to the numerous strangers who daily visit us that Reading people have got a few ideas beyond bricks and mortar".

Mr. Wheble did not wish to become involved in a dispute with the town, and much preferred to sell to the borough authorities rather than to a private purchaser. The purchase price was £1,200; he himself gave £400, another third came from dwellers in Abbot's Walk, and the Corporation's share was largely defrayed by other public-spirited individuals, and finally in November 1854 the property was conveyed to the town. Mr. Wheble certainly deserved the many votes of thanks for his public-spirited action, and by January 1855 the surveyor to the Board of Health was surveying and measuring this splendid acquisition with the aim of giving "a feature of attraction to the town". Plans were invited – with "a premium of ten guineas for the most approved design" – a sum not exceeding £1,000 was allotted to the work, the two winning plans were chosen, the relevant committee was appointed and although there was grumbling at the slow start – "this desert of weeds" it was called in June – by September the design was progressing: the ground, including the Hill, was to be enclosed by a wall with open railings, there was to be a central

Forbury Gardens, c. 1856

fountain and, in the north-east corner, a circular summer house, and the slopes of the Hill were to be planted with evergreens. By October it was decided to give it "a botanical character", and in January 1856 the last intrusive building, that belonging to the South-Eastern Railway, was removed. The garden was opened to the public on Easter Sunday afternoon 1856, and although "from the absence of vegetation the appearance of the gardens is dry and barren", several hundred visited. By July the fountain had been completed and the Royal Berkshire Band, the militia band, had begun to play in the new gardens, although it was soon found better to play from the grass than from the Hill; and by August

> "So popular and so attractive are the public gardens and musical performance become, that on Tuesday evening last upwards of 3,600 visitors entered the grounds".

It was very appropriate that these should be known as the Pleasure Gardens, and under the control of Mr. Davis, the head gardener, floral displays went from strength to strength. It was agreed that the gardens should be closed on Sundays from 10 o'clock to 1 p.m. to allow the attendants to go to church. It was necessary to have attendants as there were cases of flowers being picked or dug up, and it was hoped that "any injury by mischievous children will be immediately stopped". In fact, in 1860, the gardener in charge was sworn a special constable to help him check this, although, in spring 1861, this did not stop "parties carrying off roots of young spring flowers as soon as they are planted out for blooming".

Suttons early made an unofficial extension to the gardens, for their grounds formed "a convenient and agreeable approach to the Forbury from the centre of the town, and are freely open to the public", and it was a fair return that in the autumn they supervised the planting of a number of shrubs and deciduous trees in the Pleasure Gardens. A new feature there materialized in June 1857, when the two-ton Sebastopol gun was presented by the government to the Corporation. It was placed on Forbury Hill and by the end of the year jokers had twice fired it off in the night, breaking windows in Abbot's Walk. As a result, it was "muzzled and capped", but in March 1858 its oak carriage was blown up. However, it was decided to leave it on the Hill, and in 1859 it was placed on a stone mounting with ornamental railings.

The success of the Pleasure Gardens contrasted with the continuance of the old situation in the west part of the Forbury. The fairs were as dirty and destructive as ever, even more so since 1841 when the mayor had ordered that at St. James's Fair in July "all cattle shall be exposed for sale in the Forbury and nowhere else", so relieving the inhabitants of Friar Street and West Street at the Forbury's expense. By 1854 feeling was growing against fairs there, and after the Michaelmas Fair of that year

"There are heaps of oyster shells, manure and other refuse from the late fair which, from being exposed to the heat of the sun, emit an effluvia annoying to persons either passing to the Reigate Railway Station or to the Forbury Hill".

But not merely at fair time was the Forbury in a poor state. The 1853 proposals for improvement had not worked. In 1855, for example, the footpath between Market Place and Abbey Gateway was criticised as deep in mud, and at the end of the year complaints were repeated of roads torn up by constant traffic to the South-Eastern Railway; and in 1857 wagons got so bogged down that "the struggles and plunging of the animals is most distressing to witness". Further, timber and building materials were lying around. There was a further complication, for the demarcation between the Blagrave estate's possession and the town's customary right was not at all clear. In 1817 the town had had no option but to agree that the soil, as distinct from the surface, certainly belonged to Blagrave and Vansittart. In 1844 Colonel Blagrave's agent protested at the transfer, in 1841, of the July fair to the Forbury as "to his property without his consent", but against this Queen Elizabeth's Charter was quoted. In 1851 Mr. Appleton had been surprised to learn that the £1 rent he paid to Colonel Blagrave was for the school playground not for the whole of the Blagrave part of the Forbury, and in any case this did not override the town's rights. In 1852 both parties backed away from defining the

Forbury Gardens, c 1865

situation. In view of all this, purchase by the town seemed the most sensible move and in January 1857 the committee of the local Board of Health firmly proposed that

> "under all the circumstances of the case and having regard to the various contingencies affecting it, it would be the wisest course for the Board to effect a purchase under the Land Clauses Consolidation Act."

By September Colonel Blagrave's solicitors could report that "eminent counsel" agreed, and by August 1858 the Court of Chancery had sanctioned the sale. Negotiations continued until March 1860, when £6,010 were paid to Colonel Blagrave for his part of the Forbury, the west side of the Abbey Gateway and his property in Middle Row, and by April conveyancing was in hand.

The clearing up of the existing situation took a little time but in May 1860 the town council resolved that the fairs should be removed from the Forbury, and later that year the last circus was held there. By July a premium was on offer for the best design and in August a rearrangement of roads was suggested, but no practical steps had been taken before hard weather set in at the end of November. The hard winter put many of the poor out of work, so necessitating public works and poor relief. Thirty or forty were employed in this new part of the Forbury, but "from the hardness of the ground it was necessary to suspend operations". In later January, however, work was possible and

"a deep pit has been dug in the Forbury, where excellent gravel is being obtained, which will be required in the laying-out of the gardens".

It must have been filled in by April when the head gardener, Mr. Davis, was effectively at work. Grass was planted and the public kept off it, though not the pigs that got through the chains the Corporation had, shortsightedly, put along the edge of the road. There was some conflict of ideas between its use as a formal garden and as a place "not too good to be used", where there would be scope for public recreation and a parade ground for volunteers and militia. The latter scheme was preferred, with the whole area grassed except for the outside walks and the gravelled parade and drill ground. The formal opening took place in the evening of 16 August 1861 before a large number of people. The mayor, in his corporate robes, and with his mace bearers, observed in the course of his speech that Reading people must feel this to be

"a most suitable addition to the Pleasure Gardens that they had enjoyed for so many years"

'So many' was actually five. He also had the happy task of accepting a drinking fountain "of exceeding chaste and beautiful design", presented by Mr. William Palmer; his gift included "a clear and constant and permanent supply of pure and wholesome water", and his health was drunk in cups of it from his fountain. It was erected near the main entrance.

So the Forbury, which had figured so largely in Reading's history, was at last in the possession of the Corporation on behalf of the town. For well over a century it had been, unnaturally, divided but now, even though the two parts were separated by a wall, it was in effect one again.

VII

The Forbury Gardens: 1861–1918

So by c 1860 Reading Corporation, on behalf of the town, owned the largest part of the former abbey site. The biggest individual element, the Forbury, that old forecourt of the abbey, offered the most potential for civic development, although it was not quite as in abbey days. On the west, buildings actual or potential occupied the area beyond the new road, on the east the gardens had extended over the nave of the abbey church, whose foundations were all below the level of turf and flower beds. Although both parts were now in the hands of the Corporation, they were still divided in practice, and the main happening over the next decade or so was to be their joining.

The eastern part, the Pleasure Grounds or Pleasure Gardens, was by now well established and a matter of local pride. Pleasure Gardens and a Promenade were expected features at this time in any worthwhile town, and Reading's, although smaller than those in most comparable towns, were all that this town possessed. But possibly quality recompensed for lack of quantity, for reports were uniformly favourable, with the head gardener, Mr. Davis, receiving unqualified praise

> "The gardens altogether are very attractive as a promenade, and reflect great credit upon the taste and attention paid by the Superintending gardener"

although later generations might have had doubts about his attitude to the abbey ruins:

> "The wallflowers have this year so crowned and decorated the venerable Abbey walls that they alone are worthy of inspection".

Mr. Davis, besides designing flower-beds, kept a watchful eye on his empire; and middle-class sentiment could point the appropriate moral:

> "credit is also due to the inhabitants generally for the orderly manner in which they conduct themselves. The feeling that each person is

interested in keeping up the elegance of the grounds is now very generally entertained, and if a public garden should prove the means of spreading a taste for flowers and gardening, especially among the working class, it will repay a thousand-fold its annual cost in this respect alone".

But these early days did produce a few cases of vandalism. A girl, Ellen Lack, was caught "pulling and breaking flowers", and received 3 days' imprisonment, and Elizabeth Grove, "an elderly woman," was fined 6d. with 6s. costs for picking flowers. A man, "with all the appearance of a gentleman", picked flowers for his lady friend, but got off by paying 5s. into the poorbox: it was felt that this was a paltry sum and he was no gentleman. John Lunnon, however, received a month's imprisonment with hard labour for breaking a large branch off a tree in the Forbury: he told the gardener he wanted it for playing hockey. Most offenders were not caught:

"Some considerable depredations among the flowers were committed on Sunday last by some parties who are suspected to have visited the town by railway. This mean pilfering and abuse of public indulgence we do not think to be the work of any of our residents . . ."

but soon destruction was locally suspect; for

"during the past week several of the young trees standing in the unenclosed portion of the Forbury have been injured by some evilly-disposed party by being cut down apparently with a bill-hook"

which suggests they might have been taken for fuel. By 1864 they were still being damaged and it was firmly asserted that the offenders

"are to be found among the boys that frequent the gardens mornings and evenings"

In 1865 plants were purloined from Forbury Hill and in the next year seats there were smashed. Thereafter little was reported in the way of vandalism, which probably implied acceptance of these occasional acts and their lack of news-worthiness rather than their disappearance.

The gardens survived the late May frosts of 1865, doubtless to the pleasure of the large numbers of "townsfolk and strangers" who visited them daily. It was observed that the latter, while "united in their expressions of gratification" regretted "the very contracted dimensions of the area", especially as they considered many private gardens in the vicinity to be larger. This opportunity for a dig at the town authorities, still procrastinating over the west side, was too good to miss so, sarcastically, "we may perhaps hope to see the boundaries extended sooner or later"

The gardens continued to elicit praise, and it was fortunate that in May 1868 they were "approaching their full summer luxuriance", for

> "On Thursday they were honoured by a visit from his Grace the Duke of Marlborough who spent an hour inspecting the Abbey Ruins and grounds. He expressed very great pleasure at all he saw, and spoke highly of the place as a resource for the inhabitants of what he termed 'a spirited town'. Approval from the possessor of Blenheim is no slight compliment".

Each year the displays seemed to do the impossible of improving on the previous, but costs of £240 a year were causing some perturbation to the town authorities; and the departure of Mr. Davis, the head gardener, in 1870 was followed by the introduction of a new scheme, with a contractor responsible for the cultivation of the gardens, a keeper for their tidiness and security. Mr. George Phippen of Victoria Nurseries, Oxford Road, obtained the contract, having quoted £120 a year and accepting a prohibition on advertising and on selling plants at the Forbury; and it was agreed that the west part would be put in order before he assumed responsibility for it. Thereafter he was usually successful in retaining the contract and his work, with slight exceptions, got high praise. But praise verging on the ecstatic was consistently awarded to Mrs. Phippen, who took over on her husband's sudden death in 1893 and held the contract until 1922. A keeper was meanwhile appointed at 14s. (c 70p) a week plus 2s. a week in lieu of accommodation, a suit of clothes a year, and overcoat and hat when required. His responsibility covered all the town's holding in the abbey, not just the Pleasure Grounds.

Basic work in the gardens had been largely done, so most activity there in the decade from 1860 consisted of maintenance and small improvements, such as the installation of three lights, the renewing of paint on the fountain and fence, the conversion of the pond, now "a mass of dried weeds and rushes" to a rose garden, and the provision of new seats. In addition, the walks needed regravelling, a light iron gate was needed to keep the animals out, and a new green house was provided. Ingenious arguments were put forward for erecting a flagstaff on Forbury Hill:

> "It would be in harmony with the Russian Gun and give a more lively aspect to the crown of the Hill itself which now presents a rather dull contrast to the gay scene which the eye may rest upon in the gardens below"

This was soon coupled with the idea of making a standing there for a band, for down in the gardens crowds getting too near "had the effect of detracting from the beauty and distinctness of the notes"

and in June 1863 a flagpole, flag and band-platform for Forbury Hill were duly authorised by the Board of Health. These doubtless improved the setting for the Russian Gun, but this last could be a menace. Jokers had fired it in the past, but on a December night in 1868 all bounds were exceeded:

"By a powerful explosion of this gun the windows of the goods station of the South-Eastern Railway were broken, all the gaslights extinguished and the workmen thrown into confusion by the conviction that an engine boiler had exploded upon the premises. There were on the same night three invalids in the Abbot's Walk to whom the shock was most prejudicial".

Outsiders were suspected, and by order of the magistrates the gun was thereafter rendered incapable of being discharged. It was, in fact, a matter of chance that the gun was still there, for earlier in the year the government had planned to call in all Russian trophy guns as being obnoxious to Russians visiting England. The Hill was further improved when new wooden seats were fixed to the large elm trees there, and

"it is to be hoped that they will not be defaced by persons cutting their initials on them".

although temptation might have been avoided had the seats been of iron, like those placed elsewhere in the grounds.

The major regular activity in the Pleasure Gardens was promenading, but a favourite attraction in the summer months was listening to the band, and band concerts enticed large audiences. The brass band of the Rifle Corps – a voluntary local organization – was not at first a great success, and there were complaints in 1862 that it was always accompanied by an unruly rabble; in July of that year it was held that its drums were too loud; and in August even the weather was against them when "the boisterous state of the atmosphere" drove them from Forbury Hill to

"take up a more sheltered position in the Abbey Ruins, where a large and respectable audience collected".

The band, it was felt, did its best, but the ruins were much worse for sound than was Forbury Hill. In all these circumstances the announcement in September of the band's reorganization can have come as little surprise. Later in this decade the band of the Royal Berks Militia gave regular performances, sometimes in conjunction with the mainstay of these years, the Reading Saxe-horn Band, another voluntary organisation. Their performances were, like all others at this time, in the open, and the weather was frequently a problem. In April 1863, for example, rain washed out their performance, and the newspaper's verse the following week

> "The bright, the beautiful April rain
> Comes from the bursting clouds again"

must have seemed a poor joke to the bandsmen but a more serious impediment than the weather was lack of cash for expenses. A typical summing-up was that made at the end of the 1863 season, when the large audience proved itself very mean, for

> "the amount deposited in the box at the Forbury Garden has proved quite insufficient to remunerate members of the band for the time devoted and expense incurred".

and thereafter it seemed more promising to invite advance subscriptions towards the £35 required.

These band performances, given three, four and even more times a week during the season, were the routine attractions, but at times there were extraordinary entertainments that involved both the Pleasure Gardens and the other part, known simply as the Forbury. A major, one-off celebration was on the occasion of the marriage of Edward, Prince of Wales, with Alexandra in March 1863. The large and colourful procession, after touring the streets, ended in the Market Place at noon, and the mayor, accompanied by the other members of the Corporation, then planted a commemorative oak on Forbury Hill, and a royal salute was fired from the Russian gun there, newly painted for the occasion. Meanwhile, from 10 o'clock onwards, rustic sports had been taking place in the Forbury. These included

> "jumping in sacks, bobbing for oranges, hurdle races and hurdles, treacle roll amusement, diving for eels, apple scrambles, climbing the greasy pole, running after a pig, the bucket race, the French omnibus, ball in the ring, winding the string, donkey race, grinning through a horse collar, race up two greasy poles, etc. etc"

An ox-roasting there was spoilt when "the roughs outside the railed enclosure" forced their way in and

> "behaving more like animals than members of a highly civilized community, seized the carcase and, pulling joint from joint"

walked off with it: it was some consolation that twenty large dishfuls had already been distributed. At night there was a splendid firework display, that included the Prince of Wales's feathers, from Forbury Hill, followed by the release of a fire balloon and the lighting of an enormous bonfire in the Forbury. The whole town was illuminated, including the Abbey Gateway, which had "an extensive illumination of small oil lamps" among other decoration, and all was much appreciated by the large crowds. However, the largest crowd of the day had been in, on and around the station in the late afternoon, where the royal train stopped on its way to Osborne in the Isle of Wight for the newly-weds to receive a loyal address. People came from far and near, and

> "the whole line from the Kennet mouth to beyond the Caversham Road was covered with multitudes of people".

This splendid celebration of a national event was the last of its kind to be held in the Forbury, for the next time the area was extensively used, in connection with the Diamond Jubilee celebrations of 1897, the gardens and ruins were used only as an attractive venue for the mayor's select garden party of 3,500 guests, musically entertained in the Horticultural Society's tent in the ruins; and plans for coronation celebrations in 1902 there, were for dinner by ticket for 4,000 aged poor.

Other events held there included the firework displays, that normally took place once or twice a year. There was always, during these years, one in August in conjunction with the Reading Races, and frequently another in late autumn. Spectators paid to get into the Pleasure Gardens, but the non-paying could get a good view from Abbots Walk, where "parties of a rather rough character" might gather, or in the Forbury. The summer show could include much besides fireworks: illuminated grounds; a promenade concert and other entertainment in the Abbey Ruins; and, after the fireworks, "an alfresco ball in the old Banqueting Hall where a boarded floor had been laid down for the occasion "– the old Banqueting Hall was the Chapter House. On firework nights the ruins could show their romantic best:

> "Never were the Abbey walls so richly enveloped with gorgeous tints, or their ruined outlines so vividly developed, as by the succession of coloured fires, which the advance in chemistry has now placed in the hands of the pyrotechnist".

Organizers, of course, could plan, and illuminations with oil lamps did take considerable planning, but the weather could leave much to be desired as, for example, in 1865

> "Towards eight o'clock when the darkness of the evening gradually approached the light cast from the numerous variegated lamps that studded the flower beds, surrounded the fountain and hung suspended from the trees and flower stands produced a very pleasing effect – but

the enjoyment of those in the grounds was but of short duration, for a few minutes before the time stated for the ascent of the fire balloons, a heavy shower of rain came on and the gardens were cleared as if by magic. Of course, most of the lamps were speedily extinguished . . ."

and on numerous other occasions the weather caused performances to be postponed or abandoned.

The smoke of lamps and fireworks must have been suffered gladly, but not that of trains; and the smoke that so annoyed dwellers in Abbots Walk must have been equally annoying to promenaders in the Forbury and Pleasure Gardens. The formal complaint of August 1870 did not receive its reply until April 1872, and that gave little comfort ". . . no effort" wrote the General Manager of the South-Eastern Railway

"will be spared to prevent complaint, but . . . it is a very difficult thing to arrange that at a depot engines shall be lighted, worked, etc. without some little smoke"

Gardening activity seems to have created no nuisance. Such work must have turned up various fragments from abbey times, but no record of any such finds survives. The only recorded archaeological digging in the Gardens was in 1867 when

"a man named John Mellor has, by permission of the mayor, made some excavations in the Forbury Gardens, but nothing particular has been found".

He apparently dug twice in the area of the church, for mention was made of flint and mortar foundations, portions of "the abbey pavement", and at a depth of seven feet a leaden coffin, pieces of tile, human bones and a skeleton, but again, no further record of his activities survives.

Meanwhile, what of the part called the Forbury and still separated from the Pleasure Gardens by a wall? Although opened by the mayor in 1861 more work was needed here, and this steadily proceeded, slightly impeded by interference with domestic surface drains nearby, which had to be remedied by the digging of a "well or cesspool", 15 feet deep, on the parade ground there. The work, done under the supervision of the gardener, Mr. Davis, who received a gratuity of £5 for his efforts, involved in its levelling the removal of much topsoil and gravel, and many archaeological objects must have been scattered, unrecorded, around the borough. Organizationally, both parts of the Forbury had come under the authority of the Survey Committee of the local Board of Health late in 1861, but the wall between them was allowed to remain, a reflection of the uncertainty over the possible use of the newly acquired portion. After the initial outburst of energy, work there proceeded very slowly. A parade ground was designed and some trees planted, but many of the latter were vandalized, on one occasion, in November 1863, over 20 being damaged:

it was some slight satisfaction that the perpetrator was fined 12s. (60p.) or 21 days' hard labour. In 1864 a memorial, signed by three or four hundred, to the Board of Health, summed up the situation:

"... the smallness of the area renders it totally unfit for manly and athletic games, and at present it is in a most deplorable condition"

and children swung on its boundary chains, which were no barrier to intruding beasts which were being driven to the railway station. As the eight acres of fairground in Caversham Road were to be used as a "Place for the Recreation of the Youth of the Town", part of the Forbury should be turned into a "gymnastic ground" and the rest joined to the Gardens. These were much too small, and

"the promenade, now so limited, would be greatly lengthened, the beauty of the place much heightened, and its appearance so ennobled that the town might feel justly proud of it"

were it joined to the Gardens, laid out and fenced. Permission had already been given for the erection there of "poles, bars and other appliances for gymnastic exercises", but the memorial had no other immediate effect; and neglect continued over the next two years, justified at the end of 1866 on the grounds that it was felt "not expedient" to proceed with any alterations. From a future point of view this inertia had much to recommend it. In 1866 a proposal to erect a gymnasium there had not been followed up, and a vague threat in October 1868.

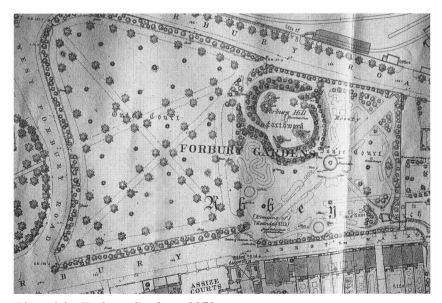

Plan of the Forbury Gardens, 1879

"That the question of utilizing the Forbury in connection with the provision of a new market"

failed to materialize. However, the crucial event occurred in 1869 when the Corporation purchased 12 acres in Kings Meadows – the Abbot's Meadow of former days between the abbey's outer wall and the river Thames – that Mr. John Weldale Knollys had put up for sale. Fortunately the proposal by Mr. Morris, that the Forbury be sold to help pay for the new property, was not adopted; and the next year the Survey Committee reported that

"as an extensive public recreation ground has now been provided by the Board of Health, the time has arrived for enclosing the portion of the Forbury shown on the plan".

By autumn 1870 this aim of adding "the old recreation ground to the gardens" had been largely realized; a new west wall to replace the chains so ineffective against vandals and vehicles had been built for some £400 and a temporary fence had replaced the wall dividing the two parts. The Corporation, partly on grounds of expense, planned

"to have the new piece of land covered with turf and not at present laid out for flower beds".

The area was temporarily known as the Outer Forbury, but its new status was emphasized when it was decreed, as the result of a complaint, that

"any circus visiting the town shall not be erected in the Forbury, but shall be sent to the Fair Ground"

and the final act came in 1873 with the removal of the shrubs and the fence between the Forbury Gardens and the Outer Forbury.

The banning of circuses from the Outer Forbury clearly marked the end of an era. They had been banned from the new garden area in 1860, but they pitched in the untidy and undeveloped area at intervals during the decade, and among them were Wombwell's Menagerie, as popular as always, Manders' Royal Menagerie, Edmond's Menagerie, Sanger's Circus and the Japanese Circus, although well before they were finally banned they were using the new circus site. In 1868 a large crowd assembled to see the testing of the new portable fire-engine – L'Extincteur – whose crew quickly extinguished a huge bonfire. There were also normally spectators in good numbers for parades there of the two voluntary military organizations, the Reading Rifles with their regular parades and the Royal Berkshire Militia with their annual parade, although training was carried out in Kings Meadow or in Mr. Palmer's meadow. A sports day in the Forbury in 1865 by the Reading and Windsor corps of the Berkshire Rifles clearly demonstrated the limited scope of the area for violent exercise when "an aged and rather feeble gentleman named Crockford" was hit by a thrown hammer, but not seriously hurt".

Over the ensuing years maintenance, renewal and small alterations took place in the reunified Forbury, now referred to indiscriminately as the Forbury or the Forbury Gardens. In 1872 plans were put forward to make Forbury Hill suitable for sub-tropical plants and a fernery at a cost of £30, and in 1874 the east entrance was improved. In 1890 a new oak carriage was made for the gun on Forbury Hill, and in 1893 a gift of goldfish for the fountain basin was accepted. In 1878 the keeper's room and shelter needed rethatching and a notice board directing people to the abbey ruins was placed at the entrance to the Gardens. Queen Victoria's jubilees of 1887 and 1897 were marked by the firing of salutes from Forbury Hill, the playing of massed bands and the planting of trees, likewise the Coronation of Edward VII. A golden holly was planted in 1893 to mark the marriage of the Duke of York, and a silver birch marked his Coronation in 1911 as George V. The attitude of authority towards the preservation of the area was slightly ambiguous. In 1886 the South of England Telegraph Company's request for permission to erect "two light poles of an ornamental character" within the northern boundary wall was refused, but three years later only an adverse vote by the Town Council reversed the Survey Committee's wish to spend £25 on creating courts in the former Outer Forbury for the recently-developed game of lawn tennis. In 1881 there had been the first of many proposals to make a Gents' toilet – "a double urinal" – there with entrances inside and outside the grounds: it was to replace that at the Abbey Gateway, but the scheme was not proceeded with. In 1911 the Reading Electric Supply Company was allowed to lay cables in the Forbury for lighting Gardens and Bandstand, but it had to reinstate and regravel the appropriate paths. In 1881 the keeper's request to sell ginger beer from his office in the gardens was turned down; and in 1914, when people were scanning the papers for war news

"If Mr. William Jackson again sells newspapers in the Forbury Pleasure Grounds legal proceedings will be instituted against him".

A proposal in 1876 that

"Nursemaids and children use the Outer Forbury without restriction"

was indignantly and successfully countered by a strong protest about its being made "a rough and common playground", and a suggestion to the Survey Committee in 1885 that there should be some slight relaxation in the prohibition on walking on the grass there, got nowhere. This prohibitive attitude was reinforced in 1904 when the Corporation stressed to the Local Government Board

The Russian Gun, c 1900

"the necessity for the Corporation being empowered to prohibit the playing of games in the Forbury, the Abbey Ruins and the Chestnut Walk".

Possibly this strict attitude had some justification. In 1874 it was felt that

"steps should be taken to prevent persons throwing paper and litter about the grounds"

but bad behaviour continued, in 1876 there was criticism of the "mistaken policy" of keeping the Gardens open till 10 p.m. a month after the longest day, for

"the result is an assembly of roughs for no particularly good purposes after dark an opportunity afforded for either injuring or taking away the flowers".

There were a few continuing instances of bad behaviour, as in 1880 when a youth was fined 20 s. for stealing roses, or in 1888 when Hannah James got 14 days' imprisonment for using bad language there: boys throwing stones, in 1915, escaped with a caution. Authority in these early days took counter-measures. In 1870 the surveyor was authorized to employ "a superannuated police constable" to keep order in the Forbury Pleasure Grounds on Sundays. In 1878 it was recommended that special constables be appointed to preserve order in the Grounds and, in 1880, that the keeper be one. A request was made in 1886 to the Chief Superintendent of Police for a constable to be there on Sunday afternoons and evenings, a request repeated in 1893 "due to the disorderly conduct of persons using the Abbey Ruins on Sunday evenings". However, authority in 1895 felt it had dealt satisfactorily with the general problem of "disorderly conduct" in the Gardens on Sundays. Only once, apparently, was permission given for an archaeological investigation when, in 1907, the Berkshire Archaeological Society asked permission to make

"some excavations in the Forbury Gardens in and about the Hill with a view to elucidate the problem of the cemetery recently discovered there".

Nothing much seems to have come of it, although later in the year the Society

"were granted permission to place a small slab with a suitable inscription over the spot in the Forbury where certain human remains have been found and reburied".

The gale of October 1881 blew down one of the large trees on Forbury Hill; and in 1893 elms had to be lopped and seats repaired there after November's gale and snowstorm; and in 1882 a tabby cat lodged its kittens well above ground level in "a fork on the trunk of a tree" on the Hill, but generally matters followed their normal course, with high praise of horticultural standards, for

"that they are appreciated one has only to see the crowds of persons of all ages who throng the seats and shady walks".

and there was general agreement that

"the Forbury Gardens are the most charming of the attractive spaces which Reading can boast".

At times claims went further, when it was felt that Mr. Phippen

"has done his utmost to make them the most effective public gardens in the provinces"

and they were joined with the ruins in spectacular evening performances.

Two eye-catching features were added to the Forbury during these years, and the first and most spectacular of these was the Lion. This was the memorial erected to the memory of some three hundred officers and men of the 66th (Berkshire) Regiment killed in a desperate fight near Maiwand during the Afghan campaign of 1879–80. Plans for a Memorial were already in hand in 1882 when the sculptor, Mr. George Simonds, a local man, suggested an angry lion. He spent some months at London's Zoological Gardens, observing, sketching and making twelve models. From the model chosen two were made full-size, and one of these was cut into nine pieces for enlargement before being cast in iron. The casting was done in Pimlico and the pieces were transported separately, for

> "the transporting of which in one mass would have formed too great a strain on the county bridges in their present state".

This might well have been so, for its complete weight was 16 tons. It was reckoned, at 31 feet from tip of nose to tip of tail, and 13 feet 11 inches in height, to be the "largest erect lion in the world" and was certainly larger than the Landseer lions in London's Trafalgar Square. Awaiting it in Reading was a terracotta pedestal, inside which were four solid brick columns, one for each paw. The successful casting of the five-ton head in August 1886 allowed plans for the formal unveiling of the Memorial to proceed. This took place in December of that year at a formal civic ceremony at which chains and robes of office were worn, with thousands of spectators present. The Memorial cost £900, but subscriptions at £1,088 12s. 3d. more than covered this, allowing, after incidentals, £106 for a Memorial Window in St. Mary's Church and £50 to the Corporation for covering the cost of repainting. It could be hoped that subscribers were not ungenerous in January 1887 when an appeal was issued on behalf of Thomas Weston, one of only 13 survivors of Maiwand: his pension was only 9½d. (under 4p) a day, and it was hoped to set him up in business as a sweep. The monument required a certain amount of routine maintenance, as in 1891 when the Lion was cleaned and painted, and in 1893 when the Reading Window Cleaning and Carpet Beating Co. was paid £1 5s. for cleaning the pedestal. However, in 1910 it required major renovation, and the £800 required for this was raised comparatively easily by public subscription. It was necessary to keep it in good order, for Maiwand day, 27 July, was marked by the laying there of wreaths and flowers and by a small military ceremony.

Space for the lion was found in the former Outer Forbury, where the footways intersected, and it was near here that the second of these striking new features, the bandstand, came to be sited. Bands, often crack military bands, were hired for gala occasions, but these years saw a steady growth of local bands performing on their own merits, numbers of performances during the summer being four or five a week by the time the first World War began in 1914. Collections were allowed to defray band expenses, but neither these nor fixed collecting boxes were more successful than in the past and, as then,

> "it is to be regretted that parties that attend the performance neglect to notice the collecting box".

The Lion soon after its unveiling

It therefore appeared a gracious public action when, between the early 1880s and 1904, the mayor or other local worthy paid for band performances. Towards the end of the period, in 1916, the Reading Temperance Prize Band, the most regular performer, was allowed to charge spectators 1d. per chair, half going to the Corporation, with no charge to wounded soldiers; but from 1918 the band retained the whole penny. Band performances attracted large audiences, but no precise records were kept, although in 1884 it was reckoned that 6,000 attended the last evening performance of the season, and that a grand total of 40,000 had attended during that summer. Band expenses for that season had been paid by the mayor, Mr. Arthur Hill, and at that last performance a vote of thanks was given and "the large company passed it amidst ringing cheers for his worship". Bands gave much pleasure, so it is a little surprising that financial support was so slight. In 1904 the Wednesday evening performances of the Reading Temperance Prize Band were financed by the deputy mayor "without charge to the Corporation or public", but at all the band's other performances that season a mere £28 17s 11d was collected.

This meanness was also visible in the matter of a permanent bandstand. Forbury Hill had become the favoured spot for band performances, but in 1880

> "having regard to the injury which has been done to the gardens by the children and others on the evenings when a band has played on the Forbury Hill in previous years, no band be allowed to play on the Hill during the ensuing summer season".

Obviously a bandstand, as many other places had already found, was a desirable amenity, but a suggestion in 1880 of

> "the desirability of the Corporation erecting an ornamental orchestra in the Forbury Gardens"

fell on deaf ears. Bands returned to the Hill in 1884 which was "generally considered to be a great improvement", but it gradually became the practice for a temporary bandstand to be erected in the former Outer Forbury near the Lion. No positive steps were taken towards a permanent structure until 1895 and then it was a matter of launching a public subscription to defray the cost. However, contributions failed to reach the £350 necessary for "a handsome iron structure" and a wooden one with a red tile roof was erected, opened by the mayor in August 1896 "in one of the brief intervals of the rain". Unfortunately its wooden floor, somewhat exposed to the elements, became unsafe and by 1909 needed replacing. The Royal Counties Agricultural Society planned to visit Reading in 1910. Concerts were envisaged as part of the activities, so at the beginning of that year the Corporation, without any quibbling, replaced the defective floor with one of concrete and asphalt. No further major works were needed on it until after the war. Of course, music was not the only noise in the Forbury, for a promenader there in February 1913 would have seen 5 aeroplanes overhead, and

> "the machines were at a great height but their strange, weird noise was distinctly heard"

Not that they were the first aeroplanes over Reading; Colonel Cody, England's pioneer aeronaut, for example, had already flown over the town.

This half-century or so to 1918 saw the town's increasing involvement in the Forbury, with the popularity of the gardens at its height. The spread of promenades and gardens was a national phenomenon and now generally accepted as a civic responsibility. The appearance in Reading at this time of other leisure-activity areas – Kings Meadow, Palmer Park, Prospect Part and so forth – allowed the staging of circuses and military and sporting activities elsewhere, with the Forbury functioning as Reading's showpiece garden. Reduced hours of work, the development of public transport and the increased wealth of all levels of society allowed large numbers to enjoy the amenities. Activity there was somewhat reduced during the war years, but band concerts continued, with many held for charitable objects, the favourite being the Royal Berkshire Hospital. Standards in the gardens in those years were inevitably lower, but there was no serious proposal to turn them into allotments, and in 1916 the Maiwand anniversary was marked, as ever, by wreaths and parade. However, in two ways 1918 marked the end of this epoch in the story of the Forbury. In January Mr. Charles Clacy, architect and Borough Surveyor, who had been responsible for laying-out the garden died. Authority then took a major step into the 20th century when, on 15 November, the Parks and Pleasure Grounds Committee decreed

"that perambulators drawn or propelled by hand and used solely for the conveyance of children be permitted in the Forbury Pleasure Ground."

The Lion and Bandstand c1905

The Lion and Bandstand 1995

VIII

Town and Abbey:
1862–1918

By 1862, as we have seen, the abbey buildings possessed by the Corporation consisted of two standing structures – the gatehouse and the dormitory of the guest-house – and the central bloc of ruins. Gatehouse, Ruins and Forbury were frequently united in gala illuminations and firework displays, but the Ruins also had a life of their own. The most regular routine activity there continued to be the spring and autumn shows of the Reading Horticultural Society, and these usually enjoyed success regarding numbers of visitors, the standard of the exhibits and fine weather. At this time the normal practice was to use the Forbury for promenading, with an exhibition tent erected in the Ruins, and by May 1867 the Society had expended the considerable sum of around £200 on a new tent

> "which entirely spans that portion of the Abbey Ruins devoted to the purpose of the show, its dimensions being 156 ft. by 90 ft."

It turned out a fortunate purchase, for the spring show of that year saw "bleak winds and frequent showers", in fact, the tent was almost blown away: however, attendance was better than feared and there were, despite the inclement season, some good exhibits. Conversely, in August 1869 when "at considerable expense the entire space of these exhibits is roofed with canvas", the show inside the tent

> "presented a gorgeous and beautiful appearance, but the heat was almost overpowering".

During these years the Horticultural Society was invoked on behalf of suggested improvements, the most ambitious of which was to erect a glass house in the area of the abbey Dormitory to the south of the Chapter House. It could, it was said, be used by the Horticultural Society, but as this would only involve two occasions in the year, it could also be used as a gymnasium and, like a miniature Crystal Palace, it could house an industrial exhibition planned for the following September, should the town hall be found insufficient. Further

> "it can be adapted as a Jardin d'Hiver, a promenade for music and many other attractive species of entertainment, all furnishing means for the return of the interest of the outlay"

which was estimated at £1,200. Although a subscription list was opened the scheme died unlamented. Six years later, in 1871, there was a suggestion that shrubs and ornamental plants should be introduced around the area used by the Horticultural Society to relieve its "dull and bare monotony" for

> "a large portion of the site of the abbey is left unoccupied and unrelieved for the whole year, and is anything but attractive to a visitor".

But no so-called improvements took place, and the Ruins remained for poetic inspiration:

> "Crumbling away!
> Past is thy day!
> And where are those who dwelt
>
> Within these walls,
> And ancient halls,
> Have joy and sorrow felt?
>
> They've passed away
> Yet dwell for aye
> In endless joy or pain!
> Returned to dust,
> Yet rise they must,
> For they shall live again!
>
> These ruins ought,
> With solemn thought,
> To fill our hearts and minds;
> To us they say,
> Earth's stores decay,
> On them fix not thy mind."

The abbey, home of the justly famous "Sumer is i-cumen in", had this misfortune of attracting mediocre verse.

Although the Ruins were spared 'improvement', some maintenance was necessary. In spring 1871 the Surveyor to the local Board of Health was authorized "to complete the repair of the walls of the Abbey Ruins with cement so as to render the same secure"

which occasioned some adverse comment on "the defacement of the old walls", coupled with the suggestion, fortunately not carried out, that

"the new plastering be hid with a sprinkling of mould to serve as a bed for the growth of beautiful wallflowers"

which hardly needed help. There were no recorded incidents of vandalism, such being seemingly confined to the Forbury; and Mr. Catchpool's request in 1880 to enlarge the aperture between the Floral Show area and "what he terms the dining hall of the old Abbey" was not granted, but if there was little adverse activity, little positive was done. In 1881 some £20 worth of repairs were needed, for

"some parts of the Ruins were falling into decay in consequence of the action of the weather and otherwise"

and complaints later that year that the prison walls were being damaged by overgrowth of ivy and overhang of trees in the Ruins and the Kennet Walk, implies that vegetation had a firm hold. Fifty pounds was spent in 1896 on reconstructing and returfing the grass terraces in the Ruins which had suffered in the Horticultural Society's shows; and £60 on moveable fencing "for the protection of the same", the wire fences, renewed in 1880, having proved ineffective. Thereafter, the early years of the twentieth century saw routine maintenance activity of replacing flints and periodic clipping of the ivy that was now so prominent on the walls. This modest maintenance programme was inevitably reduced during the First World War, but in 1915 there occurred a major happening in the history of the Ruins when the town clerk received a letter from H.M. Office of Works stating that Reading Abbey had

"been included in certain lists of monuments which the Ancient Monuments Boards for England, Scotland and Wales considered to be of national importance".

Any monument so included was, in effect, brought within the jurisdiction of the Commissioners of Works who were entitled to receive notice from the owner

"of any proposals to demolish or remove, in whole or in part, structurally alter or make additions to a monument"

This was most important as far as it went, but it did nothing to check the process of decay.

However, the Ruins were by no means isolated from the life of Reading. Workers at the Gasworks, stations, and Huntley and Palmers made a short cut through them and games were unofficially played there, the Corporation stressing the necessity of its being empowered

> "to prohibit the playing of games in the Forbury Pleasure Grounds, the Abbey Ruins and the Chestnut Walk".

There was a constant trickle of visitors and at times more formal visits, as in 1879 when the Oxford Archaeological and Architectural Society came or, in 1895, some sixty representatives of the University Extension Movement. In 1896 the Dorset Natural History and Antiquarian Society received a "learned discourse" by the Rev. J.M. Guilding – vicar of St. Lawrence's and editor of the published volumes of the Corporation Diary – during their visit to the Ruins. In the next year he took a party of some forty teachers of the Reading School Board around the Ruins, and they were afterwards entertained to tea, by the Berkshire Archaeological Society, in the Abbey Gateway. In 1898 Dr. Hurry did much the same for a party from the Birmingham Friends' Literary Institution and he frequently showed parties round, at times providing tea in the Abbey Gateway, as in 1912 when he showed members of the Reading Literary and Scientific Society over the ruins and, with his wife, entertained them to tea. Religious occasions had a place: in 1905, for example, a meeting and service were held there in connection with the Diocesan Missionary Festival. In 1910 there was a Roman Catholic pilgrimage which must have caused some public interest, for after a service in the Ruins

> "the procession formed two-deep to the station . . . and, headed by a thurifer, acolytes vested in dark red bearing a massive crucifix and lamps, the pilgrims walked to the station, singing 'Hail Queen of Heaven' and reciting the Rosary"

Other denominations held services there, as did the Primitive Methodist Church in 1914. or the Salvation Army in 1916 to mark its 51st anniversary. Conversely, plays and other entertainments were frequently staged there.

Many large-scale entertainments involved, as we have already seen, both the Forbury and the Ruins, with bands, illuminations and, possibly, fireworks. The period to 1914 was the great era of such performances. The decoration of Gardens and Ruins with "thousands of small lamps and hundreds of Chinese and Japanese lanterns" – 10,000 were mentioned for the Garden alone in 1889 – must have been a major feat in pre-electric times, but in 1909 at the Grand Fete there on behalf of the Royal Berkshire Hospital a new era dawned:

> "when the electric current was switched on and the thousand and one

coloured lamps on the various devices and on tree and arch were illuminated the exquisite and fairy-like effect produced can only be realized by those who witnessed it".

In addition, a "strong searchlight" was fixed on the roof of the Abbey Gateway

"and when its rays . . . swept over the Forbury Gardens, thronged as they were each evening with crowds of people the effect was extremely charming"

On the same occasion, the Reading Gas Co. laid mains to the bandstand and to various parts of the Ruins, especially to light the Chapter House – where entertainments were given – "with fixed, incandescent gas lamps". Earlier the Ruins had at times had their own illumination: in 1869, for example, was advertised:

"Nine o'clock – Magnificent and instantaneous Light-up of the Abbey Ruins by Coloured Fires. All the Prismatic Colours of the Rainbow. After which a grand and stupendous display of Fireworks"

and in 1889 a special feature was "the illumination of the Abbey Ruins by Greek fire". The set-piece fireworks became ever more elaborate: the Forth Bridge with moving train; Guy Fawkes with his lantern; the siege of Pekin; a bicycle race, etc. On such occasions prestigious military bands – Dragoon Guards, Royal Artillery, Yorkshire Regiment, Scots Guards, Royal Hussars, and so forth – were hired in addition to local bands, of which the Reading Temperance Prize Band was a firm favourite. Such entertainments had large audiences, as for the 5th November celebrations of 1889 when some 6,000 paid to enter the grounds in addition to the "crowds" assembled outside.

Among these gala displays were those mounted by the Reading Horticultural Society, which continued to be the most consistent occupant of the site with its two shows a year. For many years attendances and exhibits continued to be satisfactory, although both could be affected by the weather, which was too often chilly, overcast or wet. The great exhibition tent continued in use, but with very varying fortunes. In 1882

"the wind veered, got under the canvas about 7 a.m. and in a few minutes the canvas was torn into strips and about £100 worth of damage was done"

forcing the show to transfer to the town halls. In 1886 a workman was blown off the top while lacing the canvas together. In the same year the Berkshire Beekeepers, meeting for the sixth time in the Abbey Ruins, had a "beautifully fine day". They had borrowed the tent and in the evening it "was illuminated by two 3,000 candle-power electric lights . . . the motive power being kindly furnished by Messrs. Ridley and Sons of the Abbey Steam Saw Mills"

which must have been a major attraction, especially as the Ruins were illuminated only in the usual way. But from 1890 began a series of disastrous years for the tent and the Horticultural Society. In that year water poured through the centre of the tent over the spot where the flowers were staged, and visitors could hardly move about on the wet ground. In 1891 a gale "almost completely" destroyed it and marquees were erected in the Forbury, the actual show-day being fine with a good attendance. It was not repaired by 1892 when marquees were again erected in the Forbury, two being temporarily blown down in the atrocious weather. The Society must have felt fate conspired against it, for funds were low, its spring show had been cancelled and it could not afford to illuminate the grounds – Messrs. T.C. Brock and Co. provided this at their own charge. Winds ripped the tent again in 1895. In 1896 torrential rain until 4 p.m.

"depositing a great weight of water on the tent, the unwelcome fluid spouted through the central hollow almost by the ton"

and in 1897 "incessant rain" on already soaked ground made the show "a dismal failure" with visitors only "counted by the score". During the next two years successful concerts were held in the Forbury on behalf of the Tent Fund, but in 1900 high winds at 1 p.m. "completely levelled the great vegetable and fruit tent". Replacement tents survived thereafter, but worse befell the Society. Lack of local support had at times been criticised in years gone by; by 1908 there were hints that the show might cease, and in 1909 free use of the Ruins and Gardens granted by the Corporation could not compensate for the rain and scanty attendance. Poor attendance in 1910 was followed by suspension of the autumn show – the spring show had long gone – in 1911 "in consequence of the trying season we are experiencing". In 1912 the exhibits were good, the "splendid band" of the Royal Artillery played and "the grounds were, as usual, prettily illuminated" but

"the public simply would not show their appreciation of the music and promenade".

Pre-show sale of tickets had been poor, with but £45 taken at the gate, far below the minimum £100 needed. So this, the 56th show by the Horticultural Society, turned out to be the last. Shows by the Beekeepers had already departed from the Ruins, likewise, after a brief sojourn, those of the Rose, subsequently the Rose and Sweetpea Society. The staging of such exhibitions had been an important episode in the history of the Ruins, and their going marked the end of an era.

The reconstructed Abbey Gateway was meanwhile being put to quite different use. The Corporation had expended a considerable sum on it, so some return was required from letting it. Among the bands playing in the Forbury was that of the Rifle Volunteers, also known as the Reading Rifles – their official title was The 1st Berks (Reading) Volunteer Rifles – and this body became, in March 1862, the first tenants in the Gateway. The local Board of Health accepted their offer of £25 annual rent, after it had been agreed that

> "stone steps be fixed to the outside to give access to the upper room of the west wing".

Conditions for letting included the opening of the building to the public, the use of the large room without charge by the Board and the prohibition of regular band practice in any part of the building; and in November 1862 the volunteers had gas laid into the Gateway, and were allowed

> "to erect such gas fittings as they might think proper for their own purposes"

They planned to establish

> "a museum for the deposit of ancient armoury and other articles of local and general interest"

and it was hoped that the large room, this

> "very handsome apartment will ere long be filled with objects of interest which will be a credit to the town"

but nothing was done about it. The Volunteers regularly met there, the Berkshire County Rifle Association had its Annual General Meeting there, and the room was satisfactory for normal occasions, but for gala occasions it was no substitute for the town hall. In November 1870 at the presentation of shooting prizes

> "the room was crowded with ladies and gentlemen and members of the Corps in uniform. The room was very inconvenient and inadequate for the occasion"

a situation not helped by gas lighting.

Apart from some repairs to the "zinc" roof in 1868, alterations were external. As early as 1862 it was found necessary to erect iron railings to fence off the recesses at the Gateway, the Survey Committee ' erving with annoyance that "the recesses under the Abbey Gateway are continually used as urinals, to the great annoyance of foot passengers"

and ordered the Surveyor to investigate the feasibility of building a public urinal at the rear. The scheme moved forward in 1863 when an estimate was obtained from Messrs. Wheeler, the firm that had reconstituted the Gateway, for erecting a urinal and water closet with an iron entrance gate: this, the committee felt, would be "a great convenience" and the work, for some £30, was completed the same year. Around the same time a 32 foot flagstaff was erected on the Gateway roof, from which it was planned

"the union jack, recently purchased from the Reading Rifle Corps shall float daily"

The other main occupant of the Gateway at this time was the Reading Gymnasium. Victorian England's obsession with the lack of fitness of the lower classes came up against Reading's lack of a purpose-built gymnasium, so the large room in the Gateway – over which the Corporation had obtained rights – was used. Occupation began in 1867 and, although it was regarded as a temporary measure, continued there for fifteen years. After a slow start the number of members steadily increased, and competition and display nights attracted a large audience, estimated at between 150 and 200 in 1878. The room was not satisfactory on such occasions and complaints were frequent, as in 1879 when

"The attendance was very large and the room, which is badly ventilated, was extraordinarily hot; consequently the competitors laboured under great disadvantage".

All the gymnastic apparatus had to be freestanding and this alone was unsatisfactory, so from late 1885 it found other accommodation, and by the end of that year the Rifle Corps had done the same. Both organizations had outlasted the urinal. In 1869 the Surveyor was authorized

"to erect a notice-board cautioning persons against throwing stones or other materials into the closet"

but the nuisance continued and, following a complaint by Sir Paul Hunter of the Rifle Volunteers it was "altogether discontinued and removed" in 1881: its successor, slightly further away, still caused problems, but not to those meeting in the Gateway.

The Corporation still desired to let the Gateway to one main tenant, but were left with only one applicant, the Reading Abbey Club, a social organisation that celebrated its move with a smoking concert. The lease was for three years at the considerable rent of £20 a year, although the Corporation expended £10 on making various internal alterations. But by

1889 Mr. C. Outen Fulbrook, the Secretary, wished to quit it "and the responsibility, attached thereto". It was doubtless this ultimate responsibility for a building of archaeological interest that caused the Corporation to change its ideas, and accept the suggestion that the Berkshire Archaeological Society (Berkshire Archaeological and Architectural Society as it then was) should become the building's custodian. The Society was very pleased:

> "another gratifying fact is that the interesting gatehouse, formerly the manorial court of the abbot, has been granted for the use of the Society by the Corporation of Reading".

The Society got the building free of rent, rates and taxes on condition that they made it available for the public to view, and would, in the large room,

> "commence a collection of architectural mouldings and other relics of the ancient abbey, which shall become the property of the Corporation".

The Society was also to act as guardian of the Gateway, to appoint a "respectable and responsible caretaker" there and

> "periodically give a description on the spot of the Abbey Ruins"

and to conduct strangers over them. It did, however, point out that

> "these ruins would become a source of more intelligent interest to visitors if tablets were placed on the walls of the various apartments denoting their object and use".

and Volume I of the Society's Journal had as its logo a picture of the Abbey Gateway. The Corporation spent some £150 on external repairs, mainly lead for the roof, and £25 on work inside, including cleaning, but repairs, furnishing it, including chairs and gas-stoves, cost the Society nearly £40.

Good relations between Corporation and Society continued for the rest of the 19th century and beyond. Townsfolk and others received every facility for inspecting "that beautiful relic of thirteenth-century architecture". The Society's officers conducted parties over the Ruins, some, including Americans, from outside, others from the neighbourhood, including school-children and working men: it was calculated that over 250 were shown around in 1892, some 350 in 1894. The big room was "gratuitously lent for special meetings to societies of a literary and scientific character". Finally, replying to queries concerning the Abbey and other antiquities of the town engendered considerable correspondence. In addition, the Society's earlier plea for visitor-information was acted on, for "we have also to mention that our Society has furnished the Corporation with the necessary information respecting the detailed portions of the Abbey Buildings so as to affix notice-boards for the guidance of strangers".

An event of these years that gave the Society and the Corporation great pleasure was the completion of Sir Gilbert Scott's 1860 work on the Gateway, thanks to the initiative and cash of Dr. Hurry, aided by five other local worthies – G.W. Palmer, MP, Alderman Hill, Messrs. Sutton & Sons, C.E. Keyser and J. Okey Taylor. The work had been left incomplete as "want of funds left several blocks of stone and capitals uncarved". The Town Council had, in 1872, only got as far as calling for estimates, so Dr. Hurry's offer was enthusiastically accepted. The only dissenting note came from the secretary of the Society for the Protection of Ancient Buildings, who clearly had not realized the extent of the rebuilding that had taken place. New carving, he wrote, would "materially detract from the value and interest of the Gateway" and "it is difficult to see how the work would be different from the work of a forger", but this was disregarded in the general enthusiasm and the Gateway was adorned with eight carved heads on its north front, five heads and miscellaneous carvings on the south. The Corporation agreed with Dr. Hurry that the view would be much improved by "the removal of an unsightly wall together with a practically disused w.c." to the south of the Gateway. The Society rejoiced, albeit in excessive language, at Dr. Hurry's work

"in restoring the only habitable portion of the famous abbey and beautifying the home of the Society, the use of which, by the generosity of the Corporation, they continue to enjoy".

The change in the title of the Society's Journal in 1895 saw the disappearance of the Gateway logo, but this was no indication of changed relations with the Corporation. However, in 1901 the Society felt compelled to justify its activities in that it

"has endeavoured in every way to fulfil the duties entrusted to them by the Corporation of Reading in committing to their charge this interesting relic of our ancient abbey".

It continued to show visitors over the Ruins and Gateway, but not until 1902 was a start made on the Architectural Museum when a basement room was adapted to house what was, in fact, a very modest collection, and this only after complaint by the Free Library and Museum Committee. Complaints about the Society were more specific in 1904 when it was held that its Architectural Museum was "of little interest" and likewise its Archaeological Museum, in the main room, which "appears to be of slight archaeological interest and contains only a few specimens".

Terms were renegotiated: the Society was to pay rent of £15 a year in addition to the rates and taxes it now already paid, although it could charge for letting the large room. The Society's wish for a tenancy agreement of seven or fourteen years, as opposed to the existing annual one, foundered on the Corporation's demand that £50 be spent on decoration and £38 on internal repairs. The Corporation was doubtless technically justified, but the Society felt

> "that the funds of the Society ought not to be spent on merely decorative work . . . and that the cost of the decoration of the Abbey Gateway ought to be defrayed by public subscription".

So matters continued as before. The Society's reluctance to spend money during these years was understandable, for it was steadily moving towards insolvency; and although the Gateway was "the most suitable place for meetings of the Archaeological Society" it was purchased at a somewhat severe cost – in 1915, for example, the balance in hand was only 14s. 0½d. (c67p). Wartime did not help, but when the Corporation decided it could not reduce the rent the Society had to seek a new home, finding one when the University College on London Road "extended a hearty welcome to the Society": the Corporation took the Society's furniture in lieu of the cost of repairs to the Gateway. The Society's new accommodation was rent-free and aged members no longer had to toil up steep stone steps; but some regretted it. The souring of relationships is a little difficult to understand, for the Society's membership included persons prominent in the borough's affairs. What the Corporation hoped to gain is not clear, for it already had a professional museum and members of the Society, wherever its headquarters, would always show parties over the Ruins. However it was obvious that amateur effort could not look after the Gateway, and the next letting was for £35 a year with no attached archaeological strings.

The other standing building, the old dormitory of the Abbey's guest-house, was somewhat decayed. It had, as we have seen, once been used as royal stables, subsequently by Reading Grammar School, and for it ground-rent had been paid for it to the Blagrave estates. The school, in 1871, moved off to new premises in Erleigh Road and the whole of its former site was marked for new municipal development – Town Hall, Civic Offices, Museum and Library. In 1878 there was a strong movement in favour of pulling down the old buildings there. Among them was the Dormitory, for

> "its condition until now was lamentable. The old Tudor windows had been removed, and it had been cruelly disfigured in many ways by the bad taste of the last century".

It was soon saved, being purchased by the mayor, Arthur Hill, who presented it to the town. It was used for various purposes, including that of

Hospitium, c. 1885

Junior Library, but by 1891 a movement was on foot for its renovation. It was suggested that

> "the old Hospitium could be restored in such a manner as to preserve many of its original features"

as a suitable home, after repair, for the Duke of Wellington's Silchester collection that had been deposited in Reading Museum. In the event, however, it was used to accommodate the recently founded School of Science and Art that had lost part of its premises to the museum. The work of renovation and adaptation cost well over £1,500, far exceeding the £500 estimated, and the University Extension College, as it became, was allowed to make further alterations, some considerable. The Berkshire Archaeological Society was pleased with the result, as "all its original features, so far as circumstances would permit, have been carefully preserved", for "it was one of the few examples of medieval domestic architecture which this town possesses." By 1898 it had become an integral part of the complex of college buildings, opened in that year by the Prince of Wales.

However the Extension College – University College from 1902 – could not expand further on that site and in 1906 it moved, after lengthy negotiations, to a site in London Road. The Borough Council had plans to extend Civic Buildings over the former College site, again involving destruction of the Hospitium. To the Corporation's architect it was just an impediment, and

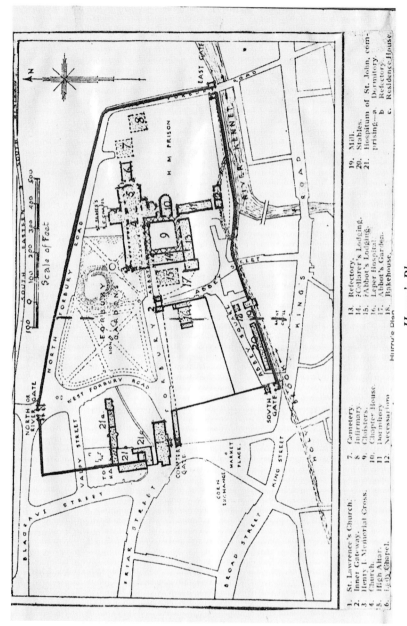

Hurry's Plan
Modern features are lightly outlined.

"That portion known as the Hospitium will probably be sacrificed with some regret on account of its antiquity, but it has been altered and patched to such an extent . . . that there is little to justify the sentimental objection to its removal. Its retention would render any adequate and comprehensive scheme extraordinarily difficult, if not impossible".

In 1904 the Berkshire Archaeological Society hoped that the Corporation would not

"countenance any destructive vandalism for the sake of modern utility".

However, during the years before development could take place other thoughts prevailed. The Berkshire Archaeological Society took heart from the Corporation's refusal in 1908 to allow the front of Berkshire County Council's new Shire Hall to obscure the Abbey Gateway, recording appreciation, and a hint

"We are glad the Corporation of Reading has acted with such consideration for the beauties of the town over which it rules, and we trust that the town councillors will act in the same spirit when they have to deal with the hospitium or other relics of old Reading".

The hint accorded with the way opinion was moving, for in that year Mr. Slingsby Stallwood, an architect and member of the Society, produced a more sympathetic scheme, and as part of the development the Hospitium was incorporated into the extended Civic Offices.

The Abbey did not lack for friends during these years, but the most prominent of a worthy bunch was Dr. Hurry, whose activities regularly received the Corporation's grateful thanks. Dr. Jamieson B. Hurry, born in 1856, was a medical man of considerable wealth, one of whose many major interests was Reading Abbey. His enterprise concerning the Gatehouse carvings has already been seen, and his fertile mind devised a number of unexpected ploys. In 1896 he produced the first modern plan of the Abbey:

"The unique and cleverly-designed ground-plan of Reading Abbey, which Dr. Hurry has so generously presented to the town, has this week been hung on the wall just within the entrance to the Free Library, and has been inspected, with evident interest, by a large number of persons, many of whom have gained for the first time a clear and correct idea of the Abbey precincts."

and he soon presented a second, framed, copy, suitably protected from the weather, for exhibition in the Ruins: his was to remain the standard plan of the Abbey for over half a century. In 1899 the Borough Council accepted from him, with thanks, a chronological chart of Abbey events also for exhibition in the Ruins. In 1900 his book, 'Reading Abbey' was published and in 1906 he presented copies of his new book, 'The Rise and Fall of Reading Abbey' to the Councillors. In March 1909 his proposal for erecting in the Abbey a memorial to its founder, King Henry I, was accepted with pleasure; and the grey, granite cross, 20 feet high, was unveiled on 18 June 1909 by the Chief Secretary for Ireland in the presence of a distinguished gathering of Reading and Berkshire worthies. The cross placed in the Forbury was near the west end of the great Abbey church. Unveiled, again at a civic ceremony, in July 1911, was Dr. Hurry's coronation gift to the borough of two tablets of Forest of Dean stone, each of over 30 square feet. They were to commemorate the first and last abbots of Reading, and were appropriately mounted on the wall of the Chapter House where, in 1913, they were joined by another of the same material and dimensions, remembering 'Sumer is icumen in', the famous canon written down at the Abbey in the thirteenth century; again Dr. Hurry was publicly thanked before a distinguished local audience at the unveiling. The mayor had further cause to give grateful thanks when, in 1915, Dr. Hurry presented 1,000 copies of his 'Short Guide to Reading Abbey' for "distribution to visitors and townspeople". His revised version in 1918 cost 3d., but

"strangers visiting Reading may obtain a presentation copy gratis on application to the Public Library".

Meanwhile his gift of oil paintings had started. The first, given in 1914, 'The Marriage of John of Gaunt and Blanche of Lancaster', was followed in 1917 by 'The Burial of Henry I'; and the offer of the third, 'Trial by Combat', was made in December 1918; these gifts of paintings were to continue over the coming years. In addition to this munificence, Dr. Hurry contributed a continuous flow of articles and lectures on behalf of the Abbey.

Dr. Hurry's investigations, and even his plan, involved no known excavation, although it is hard to imagine the Borough Council refusing permission to so generous a benefactor. Any discovery was incidental. In 1873 some old skeletons were found in digging at the gaol and another, with fragments of Purbeck marble, during drainage works in Abbots Walk: this latter must have been in or near the south aisle of the church. In 1891 the Parks and Pleasure Grounds Committee recommended for approval

"an application by Mr. Stallwood, on behalf of the Berkshire Archaeological Society, for permission to open certain parts of the ground in the Abbey Ruins, to enable Mr. St. John Hope, Secretary of the Society of Antiquaries, to make certain investigations as to the ruins".

Hurry's tablets in the Chapter House

Refusal would have been difficult for St. John Hope had promised Dr. Stevens, Honorary Curator of Reading's Museum, all help in arranging the newly-acquired Silchester collection; but nothing more is known. In 1910 a tile pavement of the Abbey was found during building operations at the gaol, and it was hoped that "Captain Wisden, the governor, will present the tiles to the Town Museum", but there was no attempt at archaeological recording, nor was there when, in 1910, the new Roman Catholic school was built in the area of the north transept and chancel of the Abbey church.

This period was, then, a very productive one in the story of the relations between town and abbey. The standing buildings and the ruins were fully recognized as civic responsibilities, and the first tentative steps were taken by the state to make sure those responsibilities were met. However, in another way 1918 marked the symbolic ending of an era, for in that year died Mr. J. Okey Taylor at the advanced age of 93. As a member of the Council, he had played a major part in the preservation and laying-out of the Ruins, had striven successfully for the preservation of the Abbey Gateway, and had been the Abbey's consistent champion against all threats to it. He ranks high among the Abbey's friends.

IX

Between the Wars:
1919–1939

The end of the war saw Mrs. Phippen still in charge of the Forbury and the abbey ruins, and her payment for the work was soon raised from £225 to £300 a year, but her two daughters, who took over on her death, lacked their mother's skills. The Borough Surveyor complained of the condition of the Gardens, demanding a full report, and the situation was not helped by the ladies' request that the maintenance charges be raised to £450 a year. By autumn 1922 it was obvious that the Gardens and contents were damaged, so in April 1923, after some, debate, the Corporation assumed responsibility, appointed a gardener/keeper at £2 10s. per week, with cottage and uniform, and decreed that supplies of plants, shrubs, etc would be obtained locally by competitive tender. Mr. Loader was appointed keeper, the Misses Phippen accepted £100 for the value of their bedding plants; and by October 1923 the Committee was gratified to report that "the grounds generally are assuming a much brighter and more orderly appearance".

Over the next few years any improvements in the Gardens were concentrated on the bandstand and its surroundings, although costly plans to improve seating and those surroundings or even to move it to a better position were not realized; all that was done was to provide guttering, pipes and soakaway and to regravel surrounding paths, although it was recognized that the continuation of band concerts was "desirable in the best interests of the public", and to have a six-foot-wide flower bed and ornamental iron fence round the bandstand. An electric cable had been available since 1923, but it was not until 1927 that the bandstand gained its electric lighting, made somewhat more appealing after 1935 when the electricity supply company allowed the bandstand's jubilee illuminations to remain at a rental of £210s. (£2.50) a year. Another eventual improvement concerned the paths. Gravel paths needed frequent maintenance, and as early as 1920 a local band had requested that paths near the bandstand be tar-sprayed "so that noise caused by people walking on the gravel be obviated". The matter dragged on for years. There was lengthy debate in 1928 when Alderman Cox felt that asphalting in the Forbury would "give pleasure to thousands", but Councillor Bishop hoped the Council would not agree "without giving due regard to the very many other pieces of work which wanted doing in the borough" a constant cry where Forbury and Abbey were concerned. In the event, "tar-paving" was carried out around the bandstand in 1930, and finally, in 1932, £500 was allotted for similar treatment of the other paths.

The focusing of attention on the bandstand was only to be expected given the role of band concerts in public entertainment. Their early popularity was great, well summed up in 1919, as "Reading people always flock to hear a military band". The band on that occasion was that of the 1st battalion E. Lancs. Regiment and despite showery weather 300 chairs at 3d. a time were occupied in the afternoon and a similar number in the evening, in addition to some hundreds of persons strolling in the Gardens. The band season ran from June to September each year and there were a number of venues – Palmer Park, Prospect Park, Coley, Thames-side Promenade – but the main one was the Forbury where concerts were given on Saturdays and Sundays and on a number of Monday and Wednesday evenings. The size of the audience fluctuated even during a concert, for there were many casual strollers and listeners besides those who paid 2d. or 3d. a chair. They had a varied fare. Military bands were expensive and rarely hired, although the occasional free performance was very acceptable, as that in 1919 by the 2nd battalion Royal Berkshire Regiment that had just returned from the front – this was on behalf of the Royal Berkshire Hospital – or by that of the 1st battalion The Loyal Regiment in 1937, Coronation year. There were many concerts by outside civilian bands; some such as St. Hilda's, Black Dyke Mills, Fodens, were famous, others, such as Don Pedro's, Harton Colliery, GWR Staff Military, Sholing Salvation Army, Shepherds Bush Silver Prize, Munn and Felton's Works, Hedington Silver Prize and many others in Berkshire and surrounding counties, had a more limited reputation and normally performed during one season only. The exception was Sonning Silver Prize Band, which performed yearly from 1928, consistently classified by Reading's Parks Authority, against its protests, as an outside band which, indeed, it was. The bulk of the entertainment was in the hands of Reading's own bands, the two performing throughout the period being the Reading Temperance Prize Band, later the Reading Temperance Military Band, and the Spring Gardens Silver Prize Band: they were joined by another regular performer whose name varied, but was the Salvation Army Band. There were many other borough bands but all appeared briefly as, for example, the Caversham and Reading Veterans Military Band (to 1926), the West Reading Military Band (1935–7) or the Reading Branch British Legion Band (1931).

Much of the period was marked by financial argument between the Reading Temperance Prize Band, speaking also for other town bands, and the Parks Authority. Bickering came to a temporary end in 1928 when the Corporation agreed to put out and take in the chairs and light the bandstand, the bands taking all chair and programme money. Local bands were in a tricky position in that they wanted to perform but felt they were getting a raw deal. Their request, in 1930, for the Council to make a grant to borough bands and to carry the cost of advertising forthcoming performances was met by a resolution that no action be taken. This was especially riling when military bands might be paid £20 or more, although lesser, outside bands might settle for chair money of 3d. per chair and a collection. Blame did not lie wholly on the Council for there had been occasions "on which the number of bandsmen at concerts had been insufficient to give a satisfactory performance" and thereafter a full complement of bandsmen had to be produced. A settlement giving £50 per season to each of the three main local bands in return for firm terms and conditions was reached in 1935 and the dispute was finally settled in 1939 when the bands had programme money, any returns from advertising and £5 per concert, reduced to £1 10d. if there was no concert "due to the inclement weather". In return it was accepted that

> "the bands appear in uniform and at full strength and that smoking on the bandstand be not allowed between items"

Most concerts were routine but, especially late in this period, a special feature might be stressed. The Spring Gardens Silver Band was strong on solos. In 1934, for example

> "by special request the boy concert soloist will render 'The Lost Chord', and there will also be trombone solos".

In July 1935 it offered, during a nonstop concert, a full range of solos –

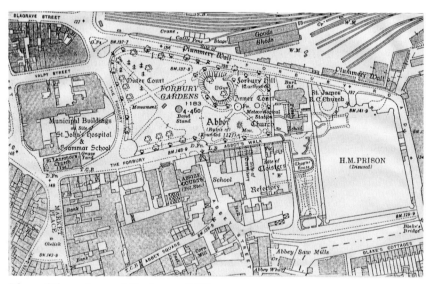

Plan of the ruins and Forbury, 1931

cornet, trombone, euphonium, piano-accordion – and "the band's male voice party will be in attendance". On at least two occasions the Sonning Silver Prize Band was joined by the Sonning Handbell Ringers, the second occasion including cornet and euphonium solos. The main regular performer of these years, the Reading Temperance Prize Band, did not lay much emphasis on its solos, and its essay, in 1931, into an accompanying display of folk dancing came to an end the next year, the reason given being the limited space round the bandstand. Not until 1939 did dancing take place in the Forbury. On the first occasion that year music was provided by an accordion band, but on the second, Reading Temperance occupied the illuminated bandstand and "despite the disadvantages accruing from rainstorms earlier in the day there was a good attendance".

At times band concerts were popular, especially when bands of high repute, like the Seaforth Highlanders in 1927 or the Royal Inniskilling Fusiliers in 1931, were performing. On the first of these occasions the Corporation paid for the band – £28 and a share of the takings – and felt that

> "the greatest publicity should be given to them by advertisement in the local press and on the tramway cars and motor omnibuses plying for hire in the district"

for the good, if rather greedy, reason that the Council proposed to charge 6d. admission, 2d. a chair and 1d. a programme. On the second occasion the band had to content itself with chair and programme money and a collection, and the grounds had to remain open to the public. But attendance at these was exceptional, and around the time it was observed that

> "bands visiting Reading are frequently disappointed at the attention which their concerts attract"

This was inevitable, for on one hand was the increased leisure, wealth and mobility in society that reduced dependence on local entertainment, on the other was the steady expansion of new forms of leisure activity, to some the decline of band concerts would have been no great disaster, for at a Council meeting in 1938

> "Councillor Dwyer asked whether any provision had been made for entertainment in the Forbury Gardens at midday Councillor. Mcilroy . . . replied that no such provision had been made. If entertainment were provided during the lunch hour it would have to be of a mechanical nature because of the difficulty of getting bands.
>
> Councillor Dwyer described the reply as unsatisfactory. The Forbury Gardens, he said, were always fairly well filled with people during the lunch hour, and it was rather pitiful to see them all facing the bandstand

as though they were expecting something (Laughter). If no bands could be provided he thought there should be a wireless installation with loud speakers or an amplified gramophone.

"The Mayor said he expected some people went into the Forbury Gardens to get away from some of the music. There was so much of it nowadays and the Forbury was a place where you could go for a little quiet".

The bandstand's neighbour, the Maiwand Lion, had survived the war years but they had taken their toll. Councillor Jackson's words, that "if something was not done to remedy the rust thereon there would soon be no lion left" were taken to heart, especially as the Lion was the focal point of the annual ceremony. However, although the suggestion, in 1931, that the Forbury's amenities be increased by the addition of an aviary received short shrift, it was a different matter when Dr. Hurry suggested a new feature. As early as 1921 he inspired the growing of papyrus, woad and flax in the Forbury and by 1924 four beds were filled with such plants, "cultivated for humanity's multifarious needs", loaned from his collection. The beds were labelled 'Food', 'Fibre', 'Dye, 'Medicinal', each plant had a nameplate, and

"as the season advances these plants will prove ornamental and instructive, and should be visited by young and old alike who will thus show their appreciation of Dr. Hurry's kindness and interest in education".

The Council duly recorded their best thanks for the loan, and next year accepted his gift of outdoor economic plants for the Forbury, but could not accept his gift of indoor economic plants, due to "the stringent financial position" and the high cost of providing a hot-house. In 1926 he moved, for health reasons, to Bournemouth – giving a final painting, 'Parliament held in the Refectory' – but still had great faith in the Council; for later that year he wrote an article on 'Papyrus', that

"may again be seen growing in the Forbury Gardens, Reading, and is well worth inspection . . . Thanks to the enlightened attitude of the Town Council the inhabitants of Reading now have the opportunity of seeing one of the most interesting of all plants associated with the history of literature".

But later that year his suggestion for expanding the Forbury display of economic plants was rejected and, although early in 1927 he opened the Economic Botany room he had given to the museum, he had no further contacts over the Forbury. Bournemouth accepted the economic plants rejected by Reading, and in 1929 Reading's display of economic plants came to an end on the grounds of difficulty in housing "some of the larger and more tender" of them during the winter, and of limitations of space. The Committee recorded "their sincere thanks to him for his great help in connection with the display in recent years", but it may be suspected that the keeper of the gardens did not sorrow at their departure.

The keeper was Mr. Loader who continued until his retirement in 1938, when the Council tried to save 10s. per week by appointing his successor, Mr. Western of Smethwick, at £3 5s. During Mr. Loader's time the gardens continued to flourish. In 1932 it was observed that "our parks are things of beauty and a constant joy"; and in 1933 Alderman Allwright "wished to congratulate the committee on the beautiful appearance of the Forbury Gardens", the mayor joining in praise for Mr. Loader, with "never have I had such lovely flowers as I get in my parlour nowadays"; and in 1936 it was felt that the Gardens had "never looked more beautiful". The weather produced its usual problems for the keeper, but none, in the event, very serious. In April 1923 a tree in Chestnut Walk was blown down and a passer-by had a narrow escape. There was a bad gale in November 1928, and in just over a year was another "great gale", with yet another in April 1932. September 1935 produced a 100 mile an hour gale, and was the only occasion in this period when a tree in the Forbury was blown down. Twice in July 1927 there was torrential rain: on the second occasion two thunderstorms converged on Reading and buildings were struck. There was a fierce storm in September 1930, fierce thunderstorms in July and August 1932; February 1929 saw the coldest spell since 1895, with the Thames freezing over, while mid-May 1935 saw a bad frost for that time of year, with temperatures in the Forbury down to 29°F, and the winter of 1938–9 saw two heavy snow falls. The one bad drought was in June 1934. Coronation Day in May 1937 saw heavy rain which drove bands in other parks to play under trees, those in the Forbury having, for what it was worth, the bandstand, although this rain was as nothing compared with the torrential rain in the next month, when 0.23 inches fell in the Forbury in three quarters of an hour.

The Forbury had, by 1919, long ceased to be the venue for extraordinary celebrations, although it could make a good starting-point for processions, as for the Victory Loan Procession in 1919. Peace celebrations there did not go beyond the temporary exhibit of a field gun next to the Russian gun. Plans, in 1926, for the staging of the Royal Show in Reading included the closure of the Forbury to the public for two or three days. Reading's Silver Jubilee celebrations in 1935 were centred on Prospect Park, although at noon on the day, the mayoress did plant a Mulberry tree in the Forbury. Coronation celebrations there in 1937 were decorous, with 11 p.m. closing, band concerts and illuminations during the week 12–19 June. Semi-official events there included free use of the grounds by the Reading Baby Week Committee for a Baby Parade in 1919, and in 1936 Reading's Peace Week concluded with a meeting there. Political meetings were in general not allowed there, but religious activities might be permitted. The Reading and District Free Church Council, for example, held an annual Easter service there and the Salvation Army met there in 1935 when General Evangeline Booth visited; meetings of the Red Cross and British Legion were also allowed. Fittingly, the mayor had the use of the Forbury in 1921 for the octocentenary celebrations of the founding of Reading Abbey. A Bee Fair was, understandably, not allowed there in 1922; and although the Peacemakers Pilgrimage held a meeting there in 1926, the No More War movement was, two years later, offered Hills Meadow instead of the Forbury. Party political assemblies were not permitted, but in 1924 the Forbury Bandstand was used

> "for instruments and loud speakers in connection with the broadcasting of the King's speech on the occasion of the opening of the British Empire Exhibition at Wembley".

This scheme did not really need to be repeated, for private wireless sets were soon available to most people, but in 1930 the Reading branch of the League of Nations Union was allowed to fix "wireless loud speakers" in the bandstand to broadcast speeches by the Prime Minister, by Mr. Stanley Baldwin and by Mr. Lloyd George. Thereafter it became a matter of amplification at local events rather than receiving broadcasts. In 1930, for example, the Reading Junior Conservative and Unionist Association were allowed to use amplifiers during their Empire Day celebrations; in 1935 a loud-speaker van was allowed at General Evangeline Booth's visit; in 1936 loud-speakers were permitted at the Free Churches' annual Easter service. The one regular occasion in the year when the Forbury was at the centre of things was when the Remembrance Service was held at the war memorial there. Shades of the past revived in 1920 when Bostock and Wombwell's Menagerie visited Reading, but it was the Palace Theatre grounds, not the Forbury that saw the show.

Few planners, however, can resist the lure of an open space. The Post Master General managed, in 1926, to get a telegraph pole erected there on a spot agreed by the borough surveyor, but more space was at risk with the 1929 scheme for constructing "sanitary conveniences for men and women in the Forbury Gardens". The scheme, costed at £1,500, was tossed around for a year or so, but once it was agreed that the construction of underground conveniences in the Market Place would not involve removal of the obelisque there, debate moved away from the Forbury scheme; and a last proposal in 1934 received short shrift. It seems a little hard that the Parks Committee, in 1936, took no action on the proposal to place direction signs in the Forbury to them.

No-one, of course, begrudged a little of the Forbury being given for the erection of a War Memorial. The peace that came to Reading, as elsewhere, on 11 November 1918, was officially celebrated in 1919, with the display of captured German weapons, including a field gun placed by the Forbury's Russian gun; and on 19 July 1919 the mayoress "planted a small oak tree in the Forbury, grown from a seed picked up on the battlefield of Verdun". One was also planted in Prospect Park, and in October £18 was allotted to providing "unclimable iron fences" around them, together with commemorative plates. Reading and Berkshire had suffered the same loss and bereavement as elsewhere, and the county regiment had been fully involved. At the first anniversary of the Armistice

> "many people in the Forbury Gardens ceased reading their papers at the time, stood up, and with heads bowed, carried out the King's wishes. Nursemaids, too, called their children to their side and kept them silent . . ."

although they had no memorial to rally around. However, the Berkshire War Memorial Committee was in existence; the planned Memorial, to the men of Berkshire and Reading, was to be a bronze Victory on a stone plinth, costing £8,000, sited near the Victoria Gate in the south-west corner of the Forbury, and subscriptions were invited. All went wrong though for the committee failed to agree on any matter, and only about £1,000 was subscribed. So by the end of 1922 the committee was moribund, £350 had gone on expenses and sculptor's fees with no plans for expending the remaining money, and the broken plaster model of Victory, later rechristened 'A figure of Peace' lay in the vaults under the Town Hall.

Little happened over the next few years, and the few suggestions made involved sites other than the Forbury. It was not until April 1931 that Councillor Sainsbury, mayor of Reading, took a firm initiative and summoned a meeting of prominent Berkshire men. All sent apologies for absence, but the Reading worthies who attended dissolved the old committee, noted that Berkshire was one of only two counties without a war memorial, and firmly rejected the idea of a utility memorial – houses for ex-service men had previously been suggested. The new committee revived the idea of a Forbury site, and Reading was prepared to spend £500 on the necessary alterations there. This was bitterly opposed by some councillors, and others felt that the time for a Memorial had passed. But Councillor Langston's peace-making contribution that

> "in addition to providing a war memorial this will make a very big improvement in one of the open spaces of Reading"

might have influenced waverers, and the great majority voted for the Memorial as planned.

Thereafter preparation of the site, including the removal of five lime-trees, proceeded quickly, at a cost to the Corporation of £260. Designs for the Memorial, the work of Leslie Gunston, a local architect, were exhibited in the Museum and Art Gallery, and the much simplified Memorial was constructed by Collier and Catley, a Reading firm:

simplicity was enforced as few further contributions came in. Finally, on 27 July 1932, the anniversary of the battle of Maiwand, the Reading and Berkshire War Memorial was at last unveiled, when "the lord lieutenant . . . unveiled a simple stone column at the entrance to the Forbury Gardens". A service was held there on Remembrance Day that year, and then, and for many years thereafter, a large section of the audience joined, from the Forbury Gardens, in the service. In February 1933 Reading Council accepted responsibility for the maintenance, repair and protection of the memorial, the Berks and Reading Memorial Committee handing over £9 11s. 5d., all that remained of their funds.

These tiny schemes, however, were as nothing compared with the grandiose ideas of the town authorities. The functions and duties of local government had greatly expanded and the existing site of the Civic Offices was very cramped; so in 1935 planning was started. Expansion on the existing site was ruled out when no appreciable part of St. Lawrence's churchyard was available, and as the feeling grew that the Corporation should develop some site it owned, the Forbury inevitably came up for consideration. Alderman Dryland summed up the feelings of many: he thought it a suitable site but did not have the courage to suggest it, for the Forbury gave pleasure to a great many people; and the mayor thought "that there was something to be said for utilizing part of the Forbury Gardens". He was firmly supported by the *Reading Mercury* and by various councillors who felt that the other favourite site, Hills Meadow, was not sufficiently dignified. Suggestions for the Forbury included one for an underground car park that, sign of the uncertain times, could be used as an air-raid shelter.

The new year began with four, soon five, sites under consideration, but the majority of the Council still favoured the Forbury for what they regarded as very good reasons: that the Council would still get its rents from the, rejected, London Road site; that only about a tenth of the Gardens would be required; that "buildings in the north-west corner would keep out the wind and improve the view"; and that

> "this has the merit of retaining the Civic Centre in the historic part of the town and in the natural place for it"

And there was some public support:

> "the site in the Forbury would be an ideal one. It is well known that this part of the Gardens is very little used, and the land being the property of the town there is no expense that way"

But opposition was becoming more vocal, stressing that the loss of even a small area of the Gardens would "spoil for ever their appearance" and, cogently, that "the Forbury Gardens were used in the summer by a great number of people who came thereto during the lunch hour for quietude and repose, and if a building were placed in the corner as suggested they would get a hurly-burly around it . . . ."

Views about the Town Council became more forthright. 'Man in the street' felt there was "enough of this foolery. Keep your eyes off the Forbury Gardens" and

"those members of the Town Council who are in favour of taking some part of these gardens for building purposes will now realize the folly of their suggestions"

The Council meanwhile pressed ahead. In January 1936 the architect's report discussed two suitable sites, but rejected that on London Road in favour of the existing site plus part of the Forbury. While he protested his desire to take as little of the Gardens as possible, his schemes included road alterations, a members' car park and, a triumph of sentiment over sense,

"one interesting approach to the suggested new municipal buildings would be by way of Abbey Street through the Abbey Gateway".

Also he undoubtedly expressed the views of many Councillors in feeling it an undoubted asset

"to have the most important buildings of the town adjacent to the relics of such absorbing interest as are contained in the vicinity of the Forbury Gardens"

Plans, tracings, photographs were submitted and a scale model requested, for the Council had approved the scheme of existing site and Forbury, which was now partly justified on the grounds that the time was not ripe for embarking on more expensive schemes. The autumn of 1936 saw continuing support for the plan from the *Reading Mercury* and from the Council, Alderman Maker, Chairman of the Estates Committee, well summing up the official attitude

". . . if the remaining portion of the Forbury is rearranged, the War Memorial moved to the Mound and another site found for the Band Stand, it would give a large space for flower beds, walks and so on. With the development of the Abbey Ruins site we could make a very beautiful garden . . . feel confident that if the inhabitants of the town realize the great advantages which would accrue from building on a corner of the Forbury, this site would meet with universal approval"

In January 1937 it was decided to press ahead with the scheme, for opposition was mounting. No reply had been made to Councillor Rowe's cogent point that it did not allow future car-parking facilities for the three to four hundred working there; and it was hoped to placate opinion by purchasing the 4,000 square yard enclosure in Eldon Square as a public garden to replace the lost 3,000 square yards of the Forbury. By now some councillors were turning against the scheme, wondering why accommodation could not be increased on the existing site; and a special committee was set up specifically to consider alternatives to the Forbury. Public reaction was becoming active, with one of the petitions against signed by more than 5,000 residents; and at least some councillors must have felt the truth of a letter in the *Reading Mercury*

"I personally wonder how any council ever thought the general public in Reading would ever agree to such a silly suggestion".

A long procedural wrangle in Council illustrated the confusion that was arising, and defence of the scheme now became carping rather than rational. Alderman Miss Sutton felt that "the people simply did not understand the matter", whereas they understood all too well. Alderman Quelch was more forthright:

"the cry of 'Hands off the Forbury' is just a sentimental slogan. It is generally understood that the site of the Forbury Gardens was once a rubbish tip. Nothing very sentimental about that".

He added that the small part of the Forbury required was insignificant in relation to the amount of Reading's open spaces and, a matter hardly likely to sway the public, that there was at present no space for councillors' hats, coats, etc. The impasse was resolved by Councillor Hunkin who, in June 1937, proposed to the Council that

"having regard to the necessity and importance of preserving the Forbury Gardens intact for public use, this Council resolve that they will withhold their assent to any proposal which would involve the appropriation of any part of the said gardens as a site for new municipal buildings"

which, after long debate, was carried by 32 votes to 12. The debate concerning the site for new Civic Offices continued, but in May 1939 any scheme was postponed until "the national and financial position becomes easier", and when it was revived in 1945 the Forbury was no longer in serious contention.

The inter-war years formed a comparatively quiet episode in the story of the Abbey Ruins, for their use as propaganda over the proposed new Civic Offices did not result in activity there. They did produce their small, but inevitable, quota of verse. One recalled the eighteenth century:

> "Splendid, though in decay, thou ruin vast,
> Gone is thy glory, yet there still remains
> Something majestic as we gaze on thee
> And muse upon thy greatness in the past . . .
> Those days have passed away and now thy walls
> Shrunk to a shadow of their former strength
> Do make a tale to form a tourist's joy . . ."

The state of the ruins is neatly described in

> "Bare-stripped rise stark the rubble walls
> And ivy clings in chapter halls . . ."

which also suggests lack of maintenance. A third begins

> "'Sumer is icumen in'
> Hear the monks of Reading chant"

which on first thought suggests a glee-club rather than an abbey.

Various activities took place there. Children amused themselves in harmless or not so harmless ways – the playing of stool ball in the chapter house, for example, was prohibited – and individuals and parties visited the ruins, not always easy to find in view of the decision, in 1923, that "the proposal that direction plates indicating the way to the Abbey Ruins be not entertained". Those not taken around could use the printed guide, reprinted in 1930, but once a year, on Whit Monday, Dr. Hurry led a party there, an event advertised in the local press, when any residents of the borough were invited to join; and on the last two occasions a school choir sang 'Sumer is icumen in' in the chapter house. After Dr. Hurry's move from Reading, in 1926, Mr. H.T. Morley continued the tradition. Official consent was given for a scatter of gatherings there, those with a religious element usually getting favourable regard. For example, the Industrial Christian Fellowship was, in 1922, allowed to hold lunch-time meetings there on five days in June; the Berkshire Council of the British Legion and the Reading and District Boy Scouts Association were, in 1926, each allowed to hold a service, and next year the Scouts were again allowed to hold their church parade there; the Reading Girls Life Brigade was, in 1937, allowed to hold an inspection and parade, a more gracious occasion than in 1924, when it was resolved

> "that the chief constable be granted permission to use the Abbey Ruins at various times until the end of next month for the purpose of drilling recruits for the Borough Police Force".

Formal music was allowed in 1927 when, in connection with the Congress of the National Union of Organists' Associations, a platform was erected "for the purpose of rendering the 'Reading Rota'" but not, presumably, political music, for at the same time it was resolved

> "that the application of the Reading Labour Choral Society for permission to give concerts in the Abbey Ruins be not granted".

That activity in the Ruins should be non-political had been stressed in the same year, when a request from the Reading Trades Council and Labour Party for use of the Ruins for an open-air demonstration was rejected on the grounds that the Ruins "be not permitted to be used for any purpose by any political organization". In 1930 Dr. Hastings, Labour MP for the Borough, was refused permission to hold a reception there to meet his constituents on the grounds that large numbers could not be accommodated; and in 1932 the National Unemployed Workers Union was consistently refused permission to meet there. These were not attempts to stifle free speech, for in all cases Hills Meadow was offered as an alternative. All this was far removed from the occasion recalled by Mr. Russell, a Trade Union officer, on his retirement in 1937, when he mentioned

> "a unique occasion when the men on strike paraded in the Abbey Ruins where a meeting was held".

Other permitted activities included filming there, in 1934, by the Reading Amateur Cine Society, who were expected to make good any damage; and, in 1928, the committee of the Christ Church, Reading, bazaar was allowed to erect a tent in the Ruins where toy balloons could be inflated for release in the Forbury.

The Ruins thus contributed to the life of Reading, but these years saw two spectacles of special importance. The first was the Reading Pageant of 1920, the inspiration of the mayor, Dr. Stewart Abraham, with historical script supplied by a well-known local historian, the Rev. P.H. Ditchfield. It provided relief and colour after the dreary war years, and the Pageant Committee had free use of the Ruins for nearly a fortnight, with permission to erect a grandstand there, with a small hut as booking office, near the Abbey Gateway. it was popular and successful and the programme gave full details of the nine episodes of Reading's history that were shown. As for the suitability of the abbey site for the Pageant

> "Its limitations were recognized from the first, and yet, except perhaps in the fight between Alfred and the Danes and the marriage of John of Gaunt, the effect has not been prejudicial. And against the lack of distance which has occasionally been realized is to be set the wonderful appropriateness of the locale, the very site of many of the incidents that are being depicted. The appearance of the battered walls with their beautiful verdure and very holes themselves all added to the vividness of the historical sense, while the entrances are well-nigh ideal"

Octocentenary tablet

Octocentenary gathering

Inevitably some damage had occurred and in September part of the Ruins had to be closed while repairs were in progress, and repairing and reseeding the banks in the Ruins cost the considerable sum of £25 7s. 6d.

Hard on this, in 1921, came the Abbey's own celebration, the octocentenary of its founding. The actual celebrations took place, appropriately, on 18 June, the day of the first coming of the monks, and consisted of a Headstone Exhibition' in the Art Gallery, which included manuscripts lent by Oxford and Cambridge; the unveiling of two paintings presented by Dr. Hurry, and of a memorial stone near the burial place of King Henry I; the performance of 'two monastic episodes' in the Ruins, and musical entertainment in the Forbury. Dr. Hurry played a major role in originating the scheme, producing a book, 'The Octocentenary of Reading Abbey', for the occasion; the prestigious celebration committee was chaired by the mayor and members of the Berkshire Archaeological Society were involved. The actual day was fine, there were a number of felicitous speeches, especially by the Dean of Winchester, and attendance was good, although tickets were expensive at 10s. for the day, 5s. reduced to 2s. 6d. for part. Dr. Hurry had earlier waxed lyrical: the abbey's record, he felt

> "will abide even when eroding time has removed the last vestiges of that *chef d'oeuvre* of architecture which Henry Beauclerk dedicated to the worship of the Almighty and in which he found his final resting-place".

The mayor's comments were rather more prosaic, that "they had a very pleasant afternoon, and he thought it was thoroughly worthwhile".

During these years few steps were taken to counter Dr. Hurry's "eroding time". Some routine maintenance occurred and some fallen flints were replaced. Landscaping, in 1922, was limited to the planting of a virginia creeper against the west wall of Reading Prison, near the ruins of the abbey dormitory. An ambitious inquiry was put in hand in 1936 when a committee of the whole Council wanted to know what alterations and rearrangements could be made to the Forbury Pleasure Grounds, Abbey Ruins and Chestnut Walk without altering their character, but all that happened was an inspection of the Ruins, and a report that

> "in regard to the general upkeep of the ruins we do not consider that any further work of maintenance need be undertaken".

There was a serious threat in 1939 to the archaeology of the area when it was agreed that shelters and trenches for children at nearby schools be constructed in the Ruins, but it did not materialize.

Private enterprise. in the shape of Dr. and Mrs. Hurry, continued to maintain the gifts they had presented. In 1925 Dr. Hurry was thanked "for having the Chronological Chart of Reading Abbey in the Abbey Ruins cleaned and repaired", and in 1930 his widow paid for the renovation and cleaning of the tablets in the Chapter House. Dr. Hurry had, before his death, presented further pictures depicting events at the Abbey: in October 1919 'Heraclius visiting King Henry II' was unveiled; in November 1922 'Selection of the Mayor by the Abbot'; in July 1924 'the Wedding of King Edward IV and Elizabeth Woodville' marked his own daughter's wedding; finally in March 1926 'Parliament at Reading in 1453' was presented after being exhibited at the Royal Academy and the House of Commons. By 1931 there was feeling that they should not be in the Art Gallery, but in some room concerned with the borough's history: feeling was, reportedly, summed up by the curator of the Museum, who observed that they

Archbishop Thomas Becket consecrating the abbey church, 1164 (Hurry)

*King Henry II and Heralius, patriarch of Jerusalem, at Reading abbey,
1185 (Hurry)*

"are generally much admired. There are, however, quite a number of
people who, for one reason or another, dislike them".

The obvious place for them was the Abbey Gateway. The museum had
long desired to take responsibility for this, and the chance came in 1937
when the existing tenancy came to an end. It was agreed that the museum
could use it as an extension for displays and let accommodation there to
local organizations in return for a rent of £50 a year to the Estates
Committee. The large room was refurbished, the Carnegie Trust made a
grant of £130 towards the cost of exhibition cases, and in March 1939
minor repairs to the paintings were authorized, prior to their transfer to the
Abbey Gateway. In the same month however, coming events cast their
shadows when the Curator's action was confirmed

"in arranging for a display of film in the Abbey Gateway dealing with
air-raid precautions"

and by October 1939 part of the borough's air-raid precautions
organization was sited there.

These were uneventful years for the Hospitium. which was routinely
maintained as part of the complex of civic buildings, but during this time
another piece of the ruins came to the attention of the Borough Council,
the so-called Abbey Wall. This was the south wall of the Abbey Refectory,
of which Reading possessed the east corner, Berkshire the rest, the land on

the north belonging to the properties in Abbots Walk. In 1926 the old cottages on its south side were booked for demolition. The Honorary Secretary of the Berkshire Archaeological Society regretted their being demolished as they were "a relic of old Reading", but observed that

> "their erection against the Refectory Wall of the Abbey has been a means of saving that Wall, which might have fallen a victim to the iconoclastic energies of our forefathers".

Berkshire wished to replace all the old cottages with police houses, but Reading owned the last cottage in the row. Demolition took place, but negotiations were protracted. By 1929, however, Reading was prepared to expend £250 on the Wall's restoration, providing Berkshire's building did not hide it, but the County's offer of access in return for repair and maintenance by Reading was felt to be unsatisfactory, although Alderman Webb's view that

> "there were thousands of people in Berkshire who, if anything was done to hide the wall, would condemn it"

was rather wishful thinking. However, by early 1931 the two authorities had reached agreement. Berkshire would not build east of an agreed line, and Reading Corporation could have access to the whole length of the wall, provided that they, the Corporation, accepted ownership, guaranteed to keep it in repair, and entered into an agreement to that effect. So in February 1931 the Town Clerk was "empowered to affix the common seal to an agreement accordingly".

Sketch of Abbey Wall cottages, 1925

Bits and pieces of the Abbey were mentioned at times during these years. Detached flints were doubtless taken as mementoes, but two were officially donated, one in 1937 to Walsingham for incorporation into an extension of the shrine there, the other in 1939 when it was resolved

> "that the application of the mayor for the gift of a flint from Reading Abbey for presentation to the 4th (AC) Squadron, RAF, in token of their affiliation to the Borough be granted".

In 1934 an oak plank was found in the Ruins, and a piece cut from it was given to Reading Museum. Some reused Abbey material was found in 1931 during repairs to the north wall of the Forbury; in 1927 skeletons were found below the floor of the Hospitium but were reburied in St. Lawrence's churchyard without any known investigation; and in 1926 abbey tile and bones were found during building operations at St. James' church. A more substantial find of twelve sculptured stones, probably from the abbey, occurred in 1922 on the new post office site in Friar Street and they were presented to the museum. None of these events resulted in recognized archaeological activity, and there is no record of any such work when the police cottages were built.

X

The Latest Phase:
1939–1991

No sudden calamity befell Forbury or Ruins during the war years of
1939–45, although the nearest bomb did demolish No. 1, Friar Street and
damage the west end of St. Lawrence's church. Unfortunately
maintenance, and so standards, inevitably suffered, although the
flowerbeds in the Forbury were not sown with salad crops, nor was a
demonstration allotment allowed there. Some wartime summer evenings
saw dancing and band performances in the Gardens, most performances
being given in aid of charities. In May 1941, for example, to music by
Mary Hyde's Accordion Band

> "the mayor (Councillor W.E.C. Mcilroy) and Mrs. H.E. Ryan will
> perform the opening ceremony and a collection will be taken in aid of
> the Royal Berkshire Hospital".

Many people were there and the band gave its services. The climax of the
wartime celebrations came on VE day in 1945, when

> "a big centre of attraction was the Forbury Gardens which were
> floodlit, and round the bandstand couples danced to a late hour, while
> others stood by watching the decorations and the dancers. Music was
> by an amplifier from which the King's speech was relayed"

the celebrations continuing next evening with a thanksgiving service
there. Pre-war standards in the Forbury were comparatively quickly
restored, for no major works were needed: in 1946 and 1965 a little work
was done on boundary walls; there was some rearrangement of
flowerbeds, and in 1957 the railings round them were removed. A few
ceremonial trees were planted, but two requests for the planting of floral
badges were firmly rejected. In 1979 a thousand Belgian begonias were
given, and the mayor performed a ceremonial planting. The main
innovation of these years was the installation, in 1958, of ornamental
lighting, with the consequent plan of keeping the grounds open until
10.30 p.m. from mid July to late September. Authority felt proud of its

achievement, but there was a little apprehension. Councillor Kemp appealed

> "to the public in Reading not to abuse this later closing of the Forbury, but to go there and view the excellent job the lighting section has done with a small amount of money".

The occasion of switching-on was marked with a concert by the Band of the Parachute Regiment, and all went so successfully that further lights were added the following year. In 1971 it was decided that, subject to sufficient lighting, the paths through the Gardens should remain open 24 hours a day.

In the earlier years of this period band concerts continued to be a major feature and the bandstand was in constant use. In 1949 it was rewired and its lighting improved, but not until 1985 did it receive a substantial overhaul, by which time band concerts were in decline. Local bands regularly performed, including the stalwarts of pre-war years – Reading Military Spring Gardens Silver, Sonning Silver, Salvation Army. When the Corporation took responsibility for concerts, these bands were paid, a payment raised, in 1947, to £7 10s. per concert for the forty arranged that year, many of which, of course, were at venues other than the Forbury. In 1950 it was raised to a maximum of £10, providing not less than twenty band members were present; but in 1953 one of the regular local bands, that of the 416 Royal Berkshire Regiment, decided this sum was too small. A small increase, to 11 guineas was considered insufficient, and the band ceased to be a regular performer,although it played an important part in connection with the Regiment's centenary in 1959; when there were two days of celebrations in the Forbury, somewhat marred by heavy rain. The Royal Berkshire's band was in effect replaced by the Reading Light Orchestra when its offer, in 1954, to give two concerts in June was accepted, the only cost to the Corporation being 2 guineas a time to defray the cost of hiring a piano. It proved popular and was soon placed on the same £10 per concert as the others; its quieter output made it the first group allowed to use "sound equipment". At times, outside bands were hired at greater cost, for example, it was decided that, in 1959, £308 be expended on the REME, Coldstream Guards, RAF and Parachute Regiment bands.

By then however, the heyday of the band concert was past. It was reported in 1949 that never more than one hundred and ninety of the three hundred chairs available were in use at a concert, a sad contrast with, for example, 1919 when all three hundred had been used. In 1956 lack of support brought about the end of concerts in Palmer and Prospect Parks and, soon after, Wednesday performances in the Forbury ceased. For some years before 1969 the choice of bands, once a major item of sub-committee debate, had been left to the Town Clerk; and that year saw the end of regularly planned performances, when it was decided that local bands could give concerts and take collections but would receive no fee. The committee regarded this as a temporary measure caused by financial difficulties, but in fact regular, frequent band performances had been overtaken by other forms of entertainment.

Other activities took place in the Forbury, but these were drastically reduced as the years passed. Religious services were held. An annual Easter service was, until 1966, organized by the Reading and District Free Church Federal Council; and there were a few occasional services, as that of the Old Contemptibles Association in 1948, the British Legion in 1946, 8 and 9, the Young Life Campaign in 1950, the Ukranian Association in 1954 or the U.N. Association in aid of UNICEF in the same year. A regular service was that on Remembrance Day at the war memorial. In the earlier part of this period it was an important occasion, with the mayor present various organizations represented and many hundreds of individuals in the Forbury and outside, although at times bad weather forced the service into the Town Hall, but from 1980, although wreaths were laid at the Forbury war memorial, the main annual ceremony took place at the memorial at Brock Barracks. There were again, in these earlier days, some formal parades: the ATS paraded there in 1942 and 44; the Borough police were inspected there in, for example, 1947, 50, 52 and 59; the Air Training Corps beat Retreat in 1948 and in 1956 Civil Defence Day was celebrated there. In 1959 Retreat was beaten by the Royal Berkshire Regiment in connection with its centenary celebrations, although it had to be performed by the TA battalion; and further ceremonies in connection with this and the handing over of the Duke of Edinburgh's banner took place in 1960. These virtually marked the end of a long tradition of military parades in the Forbury.

The grounds were, of course, used on a number of non-military occasions. There was, for example, a Savings Rally in 1946; a meeting of the Reading branch of the United Nations Association in 1947; one by the Christaldelphian Ecclesia in 1950 and a Girl Guides rally the same year; in 1962 a meeting was organized by the Berkshire May Day Festival Committee; in 1964 there was one by the Young People's Fellowship of Greyfriars church; in 1972 the Kennet Morris Men performed there. In 1965 the Reading Labour Party held an overflow meeting there when the Prime Minister addressed a meeting in the large Town Hall; in 1970 election meetings of one hour on one day were allowed to each party; and in 1973 May Day celebrations were organized there by Reading Trades Council. There were a few other political meetings, as in 1964 when the Reading Conservative Association and the South Berks Liberal Association were each allowed to hold rallies there. A few applications were turned down: the University students, for example, failed to get it in 1950 as a venue for Rag Day and in 1972 for a protest rally; a pet show was unsuccessful in 1958; the Campaign against Racism and Facism in 1978, although those refused were usually offered alternative venues. Among refusals was Old Tyme Dancing in 1950, but in 1954, 55 and again in 1967 the English Folk Dance and Song Society was allowed in. The great event of these years took place in April 1948 when King George VI, visiting the Royal Berkshire Regiment, inspected a guard of honour in the Forbury, visited the Maiwand memorial and received local dignitaries there. The next 'royal' occasion was the Coronation in 1953 when the mayor, after a civic service in St. Lawrence's church, ceremonially planted a tree in the Forbury. The observation made then, that "TV has practically killed celebrations on a general scale" was an early recognition of one major force that so drastically reduced the number of displays and entertainments there.

The Lion, cleaned up for the royal visit continued to be the scene of the yearly ceremony in July, marking the anniversary of the Battle of Maiwand. This always included the laying of a wreath, but occasionally a more impressive ceremony took place, as in 1955 or 1957 with a civic presence and the Royal Berkshire Regiment on parade. The Maiwand centenary in 1980 produced an exhibition in the museum and a service and a parade in the Forbury Gardens, where an audience of some five hundred attended. The Lion had been showing its age, and a report on Reading monuments the previous year observed that it was "chipped, cracked and rusting: weeds and lichen grow along its massive cast-iron back". The last significant repairs had been done in 1957, so although the Environment Committee rather played down the damage, suggesting that "the Forbury Lion is soiled by the atmosphere, and has a few chipped and cracked blocks at its tail end", it was repaired and repainted in time for the 1980 commemorations. In 1985 it figured on the mayor's Xmas cards.

These years inevitably saw moves against the integrity of the Forbury. A passing threat was the reappearance of a pre-war scheme for civic buildings there. Councillor Lockwood's reported remark that

> "there was not the slightest intention on the part of the committee, at any rate for the moment, to utilize the Forbury Gardens as a site for municipal buildings"

seemed to contain a threatening qualification, but nothing further came of it. Another revival from the past concerned the building of public conveniences there. The scheme was resurrected in 1959 at an estimated cost of £2,500 but dispute over the exact site – near the Abbey Gateway or near the Forbury Mound – was not resolved before the proposal lapsed. New and far more threatening, however, were plans involving the Forbury's western edge. Reading's traffic problems had worsened year by year, so the idea of an inner ring road emerged early in 1960. A small-scale plan was published, showing it running along the western edge of the Forbury, and although there was considerable criticism, its impact on the Gardens did not really register, and protest was concentrated against the demolition of No. 22, The Forbury, a fine eighteenth-cent house standing just outside the Gardens: it was demolished in 1963. Another, and growing, criticism held that the proposed relief road would be too near the town centre and it would be preferable to have it on the line of the Forbury Road to the north of the Gardens, although this was essentially a traffic solution and not specifically designed to avoid interfering with them. The Council continued with the original plan which, by mid-1966, was official policy, with the Forbury section included in the newly-christened Inner Distribution Road Stage III. The developed plan not only proposed the taking of a strip from the west side, but also the resiting of the Lion, which produced a small petition against such a move but although schemes for root pruning and advanced landscaping came to nothing, by March 1972 all was prepared for the closure of adjoining roads. Opposition, meanwhile, was strengthening. By July a petition organized by the Hands off the Forbury Gardens Campaign had gained over 8,000 signatures and the support of a local MP, and official claims "that the proposed new road would bring environmental benefits" were shouted down. Nor was there any popular support for the idea of placing the Lion on a pedestrian deck over the proposed road. Despite this the Council still considered it had found a satisfactory balance between highway and environmental needs, and although a minority of councillors were against it, it was reaffirmed as official policy. Before work started however, the context had changed, for by the local government reforms of 1974 the County replaced the Borough, which now became a District, as the Highways authority. Berkshire at first approved the current scheme in principle, but county opinion became ever more favourable towards the so-called Queen's Road alternative, which put the Forbury section to the north of the Gardens, along an improved Forbury Road. As late as January 1978 Reading recorded its opposition to Berkshire's scheme and reaffirmed that the other plan continued to be their first choice as "sound and well-tested at public inquiry"; but in March 1978 the Queen's Road scheme was finally adopted. A contemporary view that

> "Reading folk, digging in their heels with the required resolution of centuries, would have nothing of it"

probably expressed what the public would like to have done, but it was Berkshire County Council that, if only incidentally, thwarted the determination of Reading's authorities to remove this piece of the Forbury.

The main use of the Forbury, of course, continued to be as a venue for casual strollers and sitters, although the latter had, in these early years, to sit on seats rather than the grass. At times the weather showed itself adverse. There was a cold spell in 1940, when the Thames was partly frozen, and another in 1954; there was a blizzard in April 1952, and a 3-day "pea-souper" in December of that year. In 1948 rain spoilt attendance at open-air concerts, and drove the Remembrance Day service into the Town Hall. Frost and snow in December 1950 were followed by a severe gale in March. a great thunderstorm in July and a wet August Bank Holiday. The heat-wave of 1955 broke in August with a very heavy thunderstorm on bank holiday, and there was another, described as "terrific" in 1959.1n 1962 there was a considerable gale; the great gale of 1987 caused major damage elsewhere, although little in the Forbury, and likewise in 1989. Vandalism and flower stealing were trivial and, like the adverse weather, had no lasting effect, although in 1991 a small garden constructed for the blind had to be remade and the Lion, vandalized, had to be cleaned and repaired. Generally, standards of the past were fully maintained, and in the heatwave of 1955 it was remarked that

> "another popular resort, especially during the lunch hour, has been the Forbury Gardens, which are now looking their best".

This emphasis on lunch-hour visitors reflects a situation that had been steadily developing throughout the twentieth century, due to changes in work and lunch patterns in the area. And in the evening new forms of entertainment and a shift in population from centre to suburbs left little scope then for the promenading and band concerts of earlier times. However, scattered strollers and families continued to enjoy it during the day, reinforced in the later twentieth century with the young unemployed; and the abolition of 'Keep off the grass' notices in 1978 did not bring the expected spate of litter. There were hints that it was overfavoured with resources and that there was some drunkness in the afternoon, but these were not new phenomena. The situation of the Forbury at the end of this period was neatly summed up in the local press:

> "And almost hidden away at one end of the town is a real oasis, the Forbury Gardens. What a shame that when the heart of our town was being rebuilt it could not have used the Forbury as a centre piece . . . Apart from lunch-time office workers wanting to enjoy the sun this incredibly pleasant little garden hardly gets used."

It may have got a little more use than this suggests, but the days of its glory had certainly departed.

The Abbey Ruins emerged unscathed from the war, but equally untouched by maintenance. However, they had been solidly built and, generally, there was no serious threat at this time from falling masonry. Individuals visited, children played on the grass in the Dormitory area and at times parties were shown around. The earlier years saw the continuation of Mr. H.T. Morley's Whitmonday tour of the Ruins: he was Honorary Secretary of the Berkshire Archaeological Society, and had continued the tradition from Dr. Hurry's time. His fourteenth and last tour was in 1948 when "Sumer is i-cumen in" was sung by a choir from Wilson Secondary School and more than two hundred people were present. The song was again heard in 1958 in the Chapter House when it was sung by the Reading Conservative Association Ladies Choir. In the post-Morley years parties were occasionally taken round the Ruins, usually by members of the

Berkshire Archaeological Society; and the revival of interest in the Ruins from the mid-1980s resulted in more parties being conducted and informed, usually by members of a new organization, the Friends of Reading Abbey. On three occasions these tours were part of the entertainments held in the Ruins as an aspect of the publicity for the Mayor's Reading Abbey Appeal. The first of these Abbey Feasts, in 1986, attracted over two hundred paying visitors, and evoked a local newspaper headline, "The Ruins brought back to life"; the other two Feasts were held in 1987 and 88.

Other group activities took place in the Ruins. Among them, from 1946 to 1964 was a Corpus Christi procession and service. Some 2,000 people took part in a united service on Good Friday 1964, and there were other religious gatherings in 1965 and 66. Plans for a *son-et-lumiere* came to nothing in 1963 and again in 1968, and the Ruins played little part in the 1971 Festival of Reading. There were a number of dramatic performances, starting in 1955 with Macbeth. Audibility was splendid on the first two nights due to a railway strike; thereafter there was the problem of "noisy interruption" by trains. That, of course, answered the query raised earlier as to why more use was not made of the Abbey Ruins for such performances. Another reason was made very clear at performances of "The Player King", put on as part of the quartercentenary Shakespeare celebrations in 1964, when "members of the audience huddled this week under car blankets and raincoats". This had been staged by the Berkshire Shakespeare Players who, far from being daunted, put plays on annually for the next decade, the Borough helping by not charging for use of the Ruins, providing portable conveniences free of charge, and even approving the use of a horse in 1969's "Richard III". The weather was generally fair, but an unseasonable frost impeded 1974's "Merry Wives of Windsor". Since 1984 the Friends of Reading Abbey have held an annual picnic in the Ruins or the Abbey Gateway on 18 June, the anniversary of the first arrival of the monks in Reading. The only recorded archaeological activity in this area was that by Major Pogson in 1957, when he surveyed the Forbury and South Transept with his steel divining rod and "a remarkable American-made electronic device", though the positive readings he obtained aroused no enthusiasm in the Ministry of Works or the director of Reading Museum, and he was not allowed to excavate.

The Abbey was not really promoted as a tourist attraction, despite the steady and general increase of tourism in the post-war years. In a 1951 list of Berkshire's attractions it was remarked that

"the ruins of two of the most famous abbeys in the country – Reading and Abingdon – may add a romantic touch for those who have read their story far away"

but the prosaic observation in 1958 that "there were points of interest in the Abbey Ruins and the churches" was not likely to attract the non-expert. The insignificance of the Abbey in the Reading scene was illustrated in a poem of 1959:

"Now Reading seems a stolid place
No glamour in the mart of it,
But quest around and you shall trace
Small joys in every part of it
Some chapel fair
Some ruins bare
Lie hidden in the heart of it"

although in fact the Ruins were covered in vegetation. Hurry's Guide to Reading Abbey was out of print, so in 1948 a new one was issued under the auspices of the Museum and Art Gallery Committee. This in turn went out of print and soon after 1964 a draft for a new one was prepared, but it was not published; and not until 1988, when the Abbey was far more in the public eye, did a new, brief Guide, published by the Friends of Reading Abbey appear.

The war years had seen some vandalism. Repeated damage to the frames of the list of abbots and the plan of the Abbey led to the suggestion that the plan be fixed on the north wall of the Abbey Gateway, where visitors could consult it; and it was so fixed in 1949. In 1980 it, Hurry's plan, was replaced with one more up-to-date, in aluminium, based on that of Reg Ford. Other Hurry gifts, the stone tablets in the Chapter House, had also suffered, and in 1946 the Chief Constable arranged for special patrols in the Ruins "in an endeavour to apprehend the person or persons responsible for the defacement of the pictorial tablets there"; later that year Mr. Morley's offer to carry out the necessary cleaning and restoration was accepted with the Council's best thanks. Vandalism and time continued to take their toll, so that some 45 years later a major and very necessary objective of the Mayor's Abbey Ruins Appeal Committee was their cleaning and repair. New buildings in the Ruins were few and utilitarian: a toolshed in the old necessary area in 1964 and, in 1965, an "electric kiosk" for the regular supply of electricity to the Ruins. There was, however, in 1957, a flat refusal to provide, for £500, a building in the Ruins requested by the Museum and Art Gallery Committee

"for the exhibition of decorated stones from Reading Abbey offered to that committee by the Victoria and Albert Museum"

and they had to go into store. This was also the immediate fate of other carved Abbey stones found in Reading and Sonning and presented to the Museum.

The end of the war, in 1945, saw problems far more immediate than those of Reading Abbey, although the first important suggestion, that the area south of the Chapter House be made into a rose garden, rather avoided the issue; and it was not until 1952 that deterioration problems were taken seriously, when the Borough Architect reported a settlement crack "which had appeared at high level in the west wall of the east cloister". Consultation with the Ancient Monuments branch of the Ministry of Works resulted in the recommendation that the masonry breaking away be removed, the adjacent walling made good and "in due course" the ivy removed from the Ruins. The repair was done within the year, but the Parks Committee had to save the cost of £200 from other items; bad weather increased that cost by £29 4s. 6d. Thereafter no significant step was taken to arrest decay and evidence of neglect was becoming very obvious to the public, as in a letter in the local paper:

> ". . . the Abbey is being woefully neglected . . . Fences need renewing and placed in a vertical position. Rubbish and dumps of brick and earth have appeared and need carting away . . ."

By 1964 both the Inspectorate of Ancient Monuments and Buildings and the Borough's own Town Planning and Building Committee were becoming concerned, the latter recording "that it is the desire of this Committee that such ruins should be adequately maintained". Their anxiety moved the Parks Committee to obtain a report from the Borough Architect, and by the end of the year the Planning Committee included in their estimates £2000 "to enable urgent maintenance work on the Abbey Ruins" to start, and placed on record their view "that a similar sum will have to be spent each subsequent year for many years to come". But the Council referred the estimate back and it was reduced to £500.

The next eighteen months gave falling flints and considerable negotiations, but in September 1966 the Borough Architect reported that the Ministry of Public Building and Works would pay one-fifth of the cost of repairs, which he now estimated at £20,000, subject to their approving the complete scheme and the work being carried out to their approved standard. However another year elapsed before Reading received loan sanction for £10,000 towards the work from the Ministry of Housing and Local Government, and even then financial debate had continued, although the Council did recognize that the situation was degenerating: the walls were getting dangerous, repairs had been put off for many years, and it would be a Council liability should a wall fall and hurt someone. At least one Councillor wondered whether they really benefited the town

> "The major importance of the Ruins was their attraction for visitors to Reading – he doubted if local people went there often, if at all"

but given they were a tourist attraction the government could have been more generous and "since these Ruins are of such historical value, why don't we consider making a charge?"

The period of divided views and financial debate continued, with routine maintenance fighting a losing battle. The additional £150 allowed for maintenance on the flint work and the suggestion that "some remedial pruning be carried out to safeguard the fabric of the Abbey Ruins" so failed to keep pace with decay that, following a number of pessimistic reports and the fact that "the stonework condition was particularly aggravated by the severe winter of 1981/2", the Ruins were considered so unsafe that in 1982 they were closed to the public.

This marked the lowest point in their fortune, but the very fact of closure focused attention on them. By 1983 an official estimate of some £200,000 as the cost of repair and conservation was made and accepted, and later that year councillors visited the Ruins for an on-the-spot talk by experts. Complications in local finance and delay in promised support from the Department of the Environment then impeded the start of the work and gave time for expression of other views – that responsibility be handed to some other body, such as the National Trust or Department of the Environment, or, inevitably, that money available should be used on "living" rather than "dead" causes. Despite this, support for the scheme remained firm, with the repairs a high priority; a Mayor's Appeal Committee was set up; and a small pressure group, the Friends of Reading Abbey, came into being. Among its founder members were two on whom the mantle of Okey Taylor and Jamieson Hurry had fallen, as leading supporters of the Abbey. One was Dr., later Professor, Brian Kemp, who provided the historical and architectural expertise to justify the case for repair and conservation; and his publication in 1986 and 87 of two volumes, 'The Reading Abbey Cartularies', made, for the first time, a large number of Abbey documents easily accessible. The other was Councillor Janet Bond, indefatigable in promoting the Abbey's case in Council and committee; and her promise in 1986, when elected mayor, "to look after her two greatest loves, archaeology and the Abbey Ruins", was most effectively carried out, but even before her mayoralty her advocacy had aided the start of the work, for in June 1985 it was noted that

> "the early work has begun on the site with the scaffolding in place and the spraying of herbicide to remove the plant growth on the walls before working on the flints"

and in September came the welcome news that English Heritage would meet a quarter of the £292,000 now estimated as the cost.

A detailed photographic record had fortunately been made of the walls as a prelude to restoration, for

> "the walls of the ruins are in a worse condition than anticipated because plant growth has caused severe fissures, with large areas of stone (up to 3 tons in weight) detached from the main structure. This has led to rebuilding at all levels of the walls, rather than the top 5 feet as originally intended"

so that it was quite impossible to meet the original completion date of 1989. Completion was now planned for March 1991 and another £150,000 was found from the Council's own resources. Work was still uncompleted by then, but financial stringency obliged it to cease, the scaffolding being removed and the area opened to the public. The last section of dormitory wall, thus left unconserved, showed by contrast what had been accomplished elsewhere. Medieval type lime mortar had been used, and flints generally replaced as they had been, although slight changes had been made "for reasons of health and safety", mainly to prevent people climbing the walls. The quality of work under the direction of Mr. R.H. Bennett pleased both Reading Council and English Heritage, and it had been done in the face of other demands, strongly pressed, on the Council's resources. Publicity, fund-raising, conducted tours and the three Abbey Feasts held in the Ruins had, it was hoped, brought the Abbey to public attention and disproved the view expressed in 1979:

> "How many children living in Reading today know, I wonder, that Reading ever had an abbey?"

Although the Ruins, the core of the Abbey, claimed most attention, Reading was concerned with other Abbey buildings, especially the Gateway. This continued under the immediate control of the Museum, which from 1952 had the whole building, when the public analyst quitted the two rooms he occupied. As the main room continued to be let to local societies, precautions had to be taken against fire, including an external metal staircase whose installation in 1949 needed the approval of the Ministry of Works; more work was done in 1973. Internally, 1981 saw the conversion of a first-floor room into kitchen and toilets, and the outcome, at a cost of some £6,700 was a tasteful, unobtrusive and very necessary alteration. External repairs in the 1950s needed some £1,600 spent on the stonework, and in 1980 around £15,000 was needed. Scaffolding for this latter work closed the road for ten weeks and showed that closure was possible. This had first been suggested in 1974; and in 1977, at the request of the Ancient Monuments Secretariat of the Department of the Environment, a height restriction on vehicles, of 11 feet, came into force. After some inter-committee wrangling the Council. in 1982, voted for permanent closure of the road to motor traffic and so, from 16 April 1984, the Gateway was freed from the vibration and fumes that no medieval building – even a restored one – had been designed to live with.

These years also saw changes in parts of the abbey that Reading had not acquired in times gone by, the most striking of these occurring in the area of the Cloisters and the Abbey Wharf. This area had been acquired over the years by Berkshire County Council as a site for its new Shire Hall. Opinion in the town, including that of the Council, was somewhat adverse in face of a reported 10-storey building planned for Abbots Walk; so it was not surprising that Berkshire abandoned the scheme in 1966 in favour of a green-field location at Shinfield, where the County was the planning authority. During this period the town was involved to the extent that Reading Museum was allowed to organize two excavations in Cloister and Refectory areas and to have the finds from them, although the County made no financial contribution to the work. The whole site, from Abbots Walk to King's Road, then stood derelict until 1980, when the County planned to sell the site for office development. Reading Borough Council did not like the scheme, but by legislation of 1976 the County Council was, to a large extent, its own planning authority, so Reading Council approached the Secretary of State for the Environment. Among many objections raised was that it was

> "an extremely sensitive site which incorporates and adjoins listed buildings . . . which adjoins the site of Reading Abbey, an ancient monument, which lies astride two of Reading's waterways, and which is adjacent to the town's principal park".

Among objectors was Reading Civic Society that felt the buildings proposed for the east side of the Abbey Gateway were concrete boxes; and the County Council was accused of behaving like "hard-nosed property developers" in proposing a development "so out of scale with and alien to this historic site" but Reading's continued pleas for consultation were ignored and the minister declined to intervene.

The County Council had to sell the site for as much as possible, and the purchaser, MEPC, had to get their money back in development, but Reading's continued objections threatened an impasse, but modification of the proposed buildings, and Reading's becoming the planning authority, eased the situation. In this same year MEPC allowed pre-liminary excavation, followed in 1983 by a major excavation of the Abbey Wharf and Cloisters. Reading, stirred by Janet Bond, contributed £10,000 to the cost of the excavation and the mayor formally visited the site. It would have been pleasing could Reading have acquired this remainder of the Abbey site to amalgamate it with the Forbury and the Ruins but it could certainly not have matched the reputed twelve million pounds of the purchase price. However, Reading Council had, by dint of considerable effort, authorized a group of buildings that sat not too unhappily by the Forbury and Ruins: they had also contributed not ungenerously to an excavation of major importance for the Abbey's history and Reading Museum, the recipient of the many finds, played a most important part in their conservation.

On the MEPC site stood the so-called Abbey Wall, the south wall of the Refectory. This had been acquired by the town in 1930, but in 1960, in connection with the proposed Shire Hall, Reading conveyed land adjacent to the wall to the County Council, who

> "were prepared themselves to retain and maintain such wall for a distance of 80 feet from its easterly extremity and to provide that such

wall should remain visible in their future proposals".

The wall incurred the same deterioration as the rest of the standing ruins, but in 1986 MEPC, to facilitate building operations, demolished a section at its west end. This section had been rebuilt, probably in the nineteenth century, and extraneous archaeological authorities had given permission. But Reading Borough had not been informed, and Janet Bond was the moving spirit in a very strong protest, resulting in promises that the destructive work would cease as soon as possible, and Reading would thereafter be consulted, but the problem of ownership remained unsolved, each of the three bodies – Reading, Berkshire County Council, MEPC – maintaining it was not theirs. Another standing section of the Abbey evoked a protest from Reading. Soundy's Mill was on the site of the former Abbey Mill, and at its core were two medieval arches over the Holy Brook. The area was acquired by Berkshire County Council, which promised that the arches would be left free-standing. Demolition of the modern mill building occurred in 1964 when, unfortunately, the eastern arch was reduced to foundation level. Reading protested strongly and an agreement was reached that Berkshire would preserve the surviving arch, Reading would improve the condition and appearance of Holy Brook over which it stood; and an excavation was carried out on the north side of Holy Brook, in the area of the Abbey Mill, the finds going to Reading Museum, as happened after a small excavation on the south side in 1974. It was a foregone conclusion that when the County Council wrote to Reading in 1969 requesting the latter's observations on the possible demolition of the arch complex, the reply would be terse: "that this Council would resist any proposal to demolish the arches", although it refused to contribute towards the cost of preservation, on the grounds that "this Committee's financial resources preclude any assistance being given". Matters more or less so rested until 1984 when negotiations were resumed, resulting, in 1988, in the transfer of the freehold of the Arch with responsibility for its maintenance and for the adjoining banks of the Holy Brook to Reading Borough Council, the County Council making a once-and-for-all grant of £1,500 towards the immediate cost of the restoration of Arch and river bank.

Other areas where Abbey excavation took place in these years were neither owned by the Borough nor sported standing structures. The site of the Abbey Stables, extending westward from the Abbey Mill, was largely owned by Berkshire County Council and two excavations were allowed before the new Central Library was built. Reading's objections were on grounds of amenity and design, not of archaeology or the past. The redesigning of the carpark of HM Prison gave the opportunity for excavation of a significant part of the east end of the Abbey Church. Finally, during work to construct Forbury Road dual-carriage-way, a small piece of the north perimeter wall of the Abbey was found on the site of the projected west-end roundabout. Further east on the same line the wall was of other construction, but incorporated earlier material, including the carved head of a medieval ecclesiastic and although Reading owned none of these sites, its role as preserver of the Abbey was maintained, for all finds from these excavations were deposited in Reading Museum.

Epilogue: 1991–1997

❖ ❖ ❖

By the year 1991 Reading Abbey had been in existence for 870 years. For 418 of them it had been a living entity; for many of the remaining 452 it had been the victim of assault. However, during much of this second phase, there have been a few whose zeal to preserve what remained seems almost as great as the original zeal to build, and their work and influence have been out of all proportion to their numbers. The first half of the 1990's showed how necessary such activity was, for although human threats to the ruins had been greatly reduced, the ravages of time and weather still threatened, and even the recent restoration work had not entirely eliminated the occasional fall of flints and the deterioration of walls, and the last phase of the major conservation project remained undone, with the area concerned fenced off. However, the Borough authorities voted an annual sum for routine maintenance, and under the auspices of the Museum of Reading, combined direction and information signs were erected. The Museum has an impressive display of objects from the Abbey, and many more in store that are available for temporary exhibition or future permanent display. It is also supporting a project, already in hand, for the publication of its array of romanesque capitals from the Abbey. Currently, there are no major threats from building works or road improvement schemes to ruins or Forbury, although a scheme for public toilets in the latter has been revived with the closing of those in the Market Place. The Forbury continues as a well-kept public garden, the occasional communal activity taking place there, as also happens in the ruins.

It is a far cry from the era when the abbey loomed over the town, and its remains are today quite overshadowed by the buildings of a very different day and age, although commerce has contributed towards elucidating, if not preserving, the abbey remains on its site. That Forbury and ruins are tucked away has aided their continuing existence, an existence now ensured by legislation, for the abbey site is a scheduled monument. It seemed that relations of town and abbey had settled down to a period of quiescence on the lines of the current status quo, but the story of town-abbey relations is always open to the unexpected, for plans are now well advanced for major conservation work on Forbury and ruins, to be funded from local resources and a grant from the National Lottery. It would seem that some succeeding volume on relations between town and abbey will have an interesting first chapter.

Index